CITIES IN THE SAND

Leptis Magna and Sabratha in Roman Africa

CITIES IN

Leptis Magna and

PHILADELPHIA   UNIVERSITY OF PENNSYLVANIA PRESS

THE SAND

Sabratha in Roman Africa

text by Kenneth D. Matthews, Jr.

photographs by Alfred W. Cook

This book is dedicated to the Corps of Engineers,
Middle East Division, and to the men of the
United States Air Force based in Tripoli

PREFACE

THIS BOOK is intended primarily as a pictorial introduction to the personality of two towns. Today they attract only a few curious travelers, but two thousand years ago Leptis Magna and Sabratha teemed with important agricultural and commercial life. It was this very manner of life which made these cities, their surrounding province and all of Africa so important to citizens living in Rome, the capital city of the Roman Empire. Since those ancient days the rougher forces of nature have re-exerted their control over this section of the Tripolitanian coast, knocking great colonnades to the ground, bruising finely carved architrave blocks, and finally smothering all in drifting sand dunes.

In modern times a few mysterious sentinel-like stones encouraged sporadic digging for the sake of recovering an occasional strange inscription or piece of mute sculpture. This, however, was most certainly not the way to discover exactly what lay beneath the sands, and during its control over modern Tripolitania the Italian government encouraged its archaeologists to devote attention to these symbols of Rome's ancient past. For the first time scientific methods of excavation were applied to the ruins of Leptis Magna and Sabratha and eventually authoritative reports began to appear in the indispensable series entitled *Africa Italiana*. In more recent years work has been done at Leptis Magna and the hinterland of Tripolitania under the auspices of the British School at Rome as well. In a forthcoming publication, the British School will survey in scholarly detail the result of its efforts at Leptis Magna.

From these remarks it will be evident that our present little book cannot pretend to cover all the fine points and valuable details of a scientific publication. Rather can it serve only as a visual lure to attract the attention of the curious reader to a subject of undeniable value and interest.

The author is deeply indebted to John B. Ward Perkins, Esq., for his very kind suggestions concerning the text and illustrations. While studying the latter the reader should be advised that restoration and reconstruction have been resorted to by the excavators in order to offer some concept of original forms as well as to protect what original elements still survive.

K. M.

CONTENTS

PREFACE   7

1

THE ROMAN BACKGROUND OF TRIPOLITANIA   17

2

THE TOWN OF LEPTIS MAGNA   33

3

THE TOWN OF SABRATHA   48

BIBLIOGRAPHY   55

INDEX   156

MAPS

Defensive Organization of Roman Tripolitania   18
Roman Africa   21

PLATES

LEPTIS MAGNA

1. Aerial view looking east.   59
2. Aerial view looking northeast over the Theatre.   60
3. View of arches forming the southeastern entrance to the Market.   61
4. View of arches forming the entrance at the southeastern end of the Market.   62
5. Architrave block over the entrance to the court or chamber at the southeast end of the stage of the Theatre.   63
6. View along the street leading to the southeast entrance of the Theatre.   64
7. The Theatre as seen from the southwest.   65
8. Interior of the Theatre.   66
9. View showing the seats of the Theatre.   67
10. The location in the Theatre where the Temple or Shrine to Ceres was placed.   68
11. The northwestern end of the auditorium of the Theatre.   69
12. The upper stories of the Theatre's outer wall.   70
13. View looking northwest across end wall of the Chalcidicum toward the outer wall of the Theatre.   71
14. The southeastern section of the Theatre's outer wall.   72
15. The southeastern section of the Theatre's outer wall as seen from the street.   73
16. Aerial view showing the Theatre, the Chalcidicum enclosure, and the Market.   74
17. The stage of the Theatre as seen looking across to the southeast entrance.   75
18. Ruins of the stage in the Theatre looking toward the northwestern exit.   76
19. View of the stage in the Theatre as seen from the floor of the orchestra.   77
20. The stage of the Theatre as viewed from the upper row of seats at the western side of the auditorium.   78
21. View of the Theatre stage from one of the auditorium entrances in the western section.   79

22. The columned portico of the Chalcidicum facing on the Cardo. 80

23. View of the columns on the platform located in front of the small temple in the main southeast entrance colonnade of the Chalcidicum. 81

24. The main southeast colonnade of the Chalcidicum entrance. 82

25. The Arch of Trajan as seen from the southwest, spanning the Cardo. 83

26. View looking northeast along the Cardo to the Arch of Trajan and the Arch of Tiberius. 84

27. The western pool in the *frigidarium* of the Hadrianic Baths. 85

28. Detail of the stone archway over the entrance to the pool in the *tepidarium* of the Hadrianic Baths. 86

29. The latrine in the northeast corner of the Hadrianic Baths. 87

30. View of the Palaestra in front of the Hadrianic Baths. 88

31. Eastern end of the Palaestra. 89

32. View looking northwest along the street leading to the four-way Arch of Septimius Severus. 90

33. The southwestern side of the four-way Arch of Septimius Severus. 91

34. The southwestern side of the four-way Arch of Septimius Severus, showing the Arch of Trajan in the distance. 92

35. Inscription to Augusta Salutaris atop the northwest wall of the Cardo. 93

36. A closer view of the inscription to Augusta Salutaris. 94

37. Interior of the Severan Forum looking toward the Basilica at the northeast end. 95

38. The reconstituted arches of the southeastern section of the colonnade surrounding the Severan Forum. 96

39. One of the Gorgon heads on the southeastern arcade of the Severan Forum. 97

40. View looking toward the southeastern apse of the Severan Basilica. 98

41. Interior of the Severan Basilica. 99

42. A portion of the northeastern colonnade of the Severan Basilica. 100

SABRATHA

43. View looking eastward along the coast. 101

44. Aerial view showing the Theatre, the Temple of Isis, the Forum, and the courtyard of the Antonine Temple. 102

45. Aerial view looking westward. 103

46. The Forum looking toward the southwest end. 104

47. Columns standing on the southeast wall of the podium of the East Forum Temple, and columns from the Forum's southeast portico. 105

48. Columns on the southeast podium wall of the East Forum Temple as seen from the inside of the podium. 106

49. The Forum as seen looking northwest over the adjacent ruins. 107

50. View looking northwest toward the Forum. 108

51. The opening or gate in the Byzantine wall. 109

52. The sunken court and surrounding colonnade of a private house. 110

53. View looking northeast toward the Theatre. 111

54. The southwestern wall of the Theatre auditorium. 112

55. View of the supporting walls and corridors beneath the seats of the Theatre. 113

56. Interior of the Theatre auditorium. 114

57. Aerial view of the Theatre from the southeast. 115

58. The Theatre as viewed from the southwest. 116

59. View looking northeast from the seating area of the Theatre. 117

60. The exterior wall of the Theatre auditorium as seen from the west. 118

61. The southwestern section of the auditorium wall of the Theatre. 119

62. View into the peripheral corridor beneath the seats on the western side of the Theatre. 120

63. The west end of the *scaenae frons* of the Theatre. 121

64. The Theatre as seen from the south. 122

65. The west face of the Theatre auditorium. 123

66. View looking north through the ruins of the seats in the auditorium toward the *scaenae frons* of the Theatre. 124

67. Looking northwest toward the stage of the Theatre. 125

68. The *scaenae frons*, the stage, and the orchestra of the Theatre. 126

69. The stage of the Theatre viewed from its western end. 127

70. A decorated niche in the supporting wall along the front of the stage in the Theatre. 128

71. Decorative frieze along the supporting wall of the Theatre stage. 129

13

ART TREASURES FROM LEPTIS MAGNA AND SABRATHA

72. Antinous-like statue from the Hadrianic Baths (Leptis Magna).   130
73. Statue of Artemis of Ephesus (Leptis Magna).   131
74. Imperial statue showing close view of the detail on the cuirass (Leptis Magna).   132
75. Marble statue of a goddess (Leptis Magna).   133
76. Marble portrait heads for insertion in statues (Leptis Magna).   134
77. Marble statue of a god or hero.   135
78. Marble statues and a Punic inscription (Leptis Magna).   136
79. Marble statue of Athena (Leptis Magna).   137
80. Marble statue of a god (Leptis Magna).   138
81. Statue of Aphrodite (Leptis Magna).   139
82. Marble portrait statue of a magistrate (Leptis Magna).   140
83. Reconstruction of the Exedra of Septimius Severus (Leptis Magna).   141
84. Mosaic, fragments of statues, and portrait heads (Leptis Magna).   142
85. Mosaic from the region just to the north of the Palaestra (Leptis Magna).   143
86. Portrait head of Augustus (Leptis Magna).   144
87. Portrait head of Tiberius (Leptis Magna).   145
88. Julio-Claudian portrait head.   146
89. A group of three marble statues (Leptis Magna).   147
90. Mosaic.   148
91. Mosaic (Sabratha).   149
92. Mosaic decoration from the Oceanus Baths (Sabratha).   150
93. Mosaics (Sabratha).   151
94. Bust of the goddess Concordia (Sabratha).   152
95. Statue of the goddess Coelestis (Sabratha).   153
96. Mosaics and column bases from the Justinianic Basilica (Sabratha).   154
97. Mosaic from the Justinianic Basilica (Sabratha).   155

CITIES IN THE SAND

Leptis Magna and Sabratha in Roman Africa

1

THE ROMAN BACKGROUND OF TRIPOLITANIA*

WHETHER OR NOT it is true that Publius Cornelius Scipio Aemilianus Minor wept as he studied the destruction which he had wrought on Carthage in 146 B.C., it is certain that the Roman government was not prepared to comprehend the vast implications of his success. With the spoils of conquest now in hand the officials in Rome had to decide what was to be done with this African land which was now fully theirs. Of course, their initial concern was with Carthage, whose very existence had induced the planning of Scipio's punitive expedition. Having decided at last to retain the territory surrounding Carthage, which had originally belonged to the government and citizens of that town, the republican government at Rome renamed this area the Roman province of Africa. Punic holdings along the north coast to the west of Carthage were ceded to the faithful city of Utica. To the southeast of Carthage lay a long stretch of coast reaching south from Hadrumetum and then east toward the Sirtic gulf. This coastal plain and the adjacent hinterland were turned over to Masinissa, the king of Numidia and a friend of Rome. By this division Rome retained for itself the most civilized portion of this section of Africa and proceeded to manage it by installing a Roman governor at Utica. As for the new coastal lands given to Numidia, the agricultural and commercial potential of such towns as Leptis Magna, Oea (Tripoli), and Sabratha was evidently left in slow development under the rule of Masinissa.

In actuality Masinissa had already come into the possession of these towns just prior to the outbreak of the third Punic war, attracted to them by the promise which they offered of lucrative overseas trade. Originally settled as Phoenician trading stations serving as contact points on the coast for trade with native tribes further inland, Sabratha, Oea (Tripoli), and Leptis Magna gradually passed into the control of Carthage when the Assyrians seized the country of Phoenicia in the late eighth century B.C. In time the original bonds of culture and religion gave way to those of a more political nature, and by the end of the sixth century B.C. these three towns were no longer independent but had been incorporated into the Carthaginian empire. As important commercial centers they became known as the Emporia, from the Greek word *emporion,* meaning a commercial post. Although their relations with the exter-

* Throughout this text the reader will notice a variation in the spelling of the territory in which Leptis Magna, Oea, and Sabratha are located. "Tripolitania" is a modernization of the Romano-Byzantine name "Tripolitana" given to this area by virtue of its three important cities. Prior to the end of the third century A.D. no such name was used in official records of the province. However, the author has taken the liberty of using the spelling "Tripolitania" on occasions to simplify geographical references and to associate the area with a term still to be seen on modern maps.

17

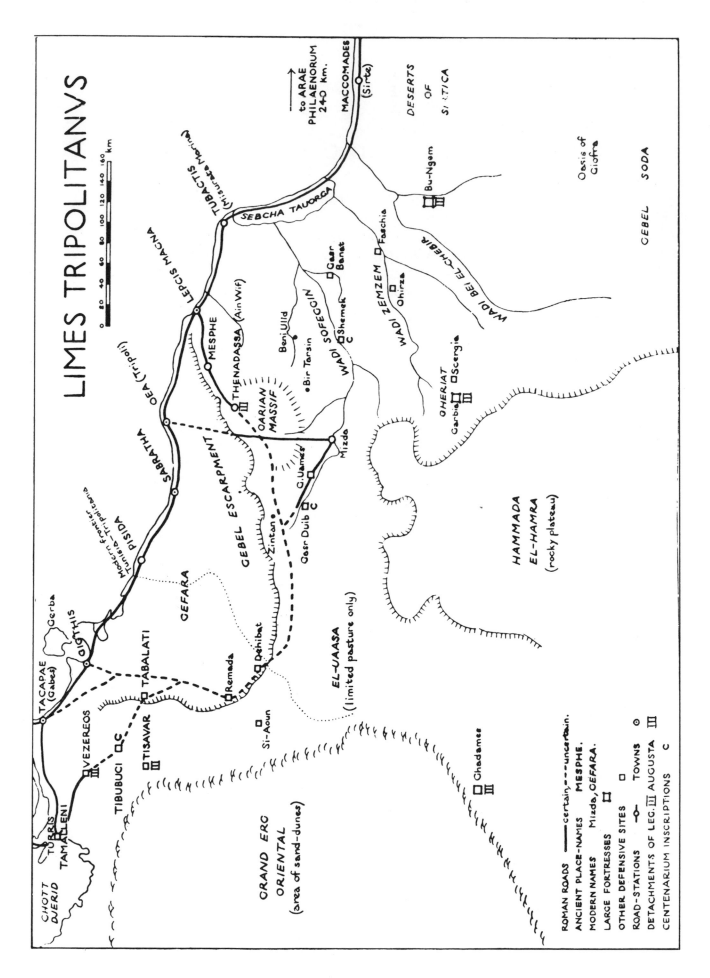

Defensive Organization of Roman Tripolitania.

nal world were controlled by Carthage, their internal affairs must have been left largely in their own hands. On the basis of its original Phoenician constitution Leptis Magna, and most probably Oea and Sabratha as well, maintained a senate or assembly and two principal magistrates, the *suphetes,* elected annually. The maintenance of ships of war and armies was denied these cities and they were compelled to depend on Carthage for their military defence. In return for this they guaranteed to supply Carthage with food, recruits, and money when necessary.

At the conclusion of the second Punic war in 202 B.C. Carthage lost her overseas holdings and was compelled to surrender to the newly-established kingdom of Numidia much of the African territory which the Numidian ruler Masinissa claimed. The cities of the Emporia, however, were left under Carthaginian control and the government must have continued much as before. Even when Carthage became an ally of Rome a few years later, and thus a Roman dependency with certain continuing obligations, the form of internal government cannot have changed. Nor was there probably any change when Masinissa, after several years of gradual encroachment, was finally confirmed in his possession of the cities of the Emporia at the conclusion of the third Punic war in 146 B.C. With the Numidian government centered at Cirta, to the west beyond the new Roman province of Africa, Leptis and Sabratha must have been left relatively unhampered in their government. Since Numidia was actually a client kingdom, however, subservient to Rome in all important matters, the Emporia also must have felt the Roman influence.

In 112 B.C. dynastic problems arose in Numidia, and the Roman Senate, obliged to protect the rights of its allies Hiempsal and Adherbal as heirs to the Numidian throne, declared war on Jugurtha, who also aspired to the throne as sole ruler. When this war, known as the Jugurthine war, ended in 106 B.C. Rome divided the Numidian territories between Bocchus, the king of Mauretania, and Gauda, the single surviving heir to the Numidian throne after the assassination of the immediate heirs by Jugurtha. Leptis Magna, however, and possibly Oea and Sabratha as well, were added to the Roman province, and from this period local government must have been controlled indirectly by Rome.

With the cessation of hostilities in 106 B.C. the inhabitants of Roman Africa turned once more to their agricultural pursuits, specializing in wheat, olives, and grapes. From the proconsular status of the governor, now resident at Carthage, the province was known as Africa Proconsularis, and during the peace of the early first century B.C. it revealed the promise of great agricultural wealth for which it later became famous. Leptis Magna turned particular attention to increasing the production of olive oil, while both wheat and oil became the major products of the province in general. Vast quantities of these were assessed by the government at Rome and during this first century B.C. Africa became one of the major sources of supply for the grain dole to the populace of Rome. In 46 B.C. Julius Caesar entered Africa to

19

engage the remaining Pompeian forces who had threatened his position during the civil war between himself and Pompey. On the field at Thapsus Caesar defeated his enemies, among whom were numbered soldiers of the Numidian king Juba. Following this victory Caesar reorganized all of the Roman territories in Africa. Africa Proconsularis, now called Africa Vetus, was left as it had already been established. New arrangements, however, were necessary for the kingdom of Numidia, which had obviously come to disregard its responsibility as a client kingdom functioning to protect the coastal territories from the desert tribes. Juba, its king, had supported Pompey. Therefore the kingdom of Numidia was abolished, and the territory formed into the new province of Africa Nova, an adjunct to Africa Vetus. At the conclusion of these arrangements Caesar placed on Africa an annual levy of 200,000 Attic medimni of wheat and three million librae of oil. Thus Leptis Magna, Sabratha, and Oea had passed by diverse stages from Punic commercial posts of Carthage through phases of Numidian control and into the expanding imperial authority of Rome.

Although the emperor Augustus never visited Africa himself he ordered a reorganization of the provinces there during his visit to Spain in 25 B.C. In 27 B.C. he had already assigned Africa to the Roman Senate as one of the provinces to be administered by that body. Two years later he directed that an official of consular or praetorian rank be appointed as proconsul to govern the province. It was highly unusual that the Senate should be given this particular authority. Earlier Augustus had married the young Numidian prince Juba II, brought up in Rome as a hostage, to Cleopatra Selene, daughter of Antony and Cleopatra. Then Augustus reestablished the client kingdom of Numidia and installed Juba as king. In 25 B.C., however, his consideration of the African situation led him to transfer Juba to the throne of Mauretania and reincorporate Numidia into the province of Africa, which now stretched from the Ampsaga River on the coast above Cirta to the western limits of Cyrenaica.

The unsettled conditions of the interior led Augustus to station the Third Augustan Legion in the province and it was the presence of this military force in an area subject to the authority of the Roman Senate which was so unusual. It was Augustus' general policy to retain in his own power those sections of the empire which required military establishments. During this early period the legate of the legion in Africa was subordinate to the Roman governor now resident at Carthage. The Third Augustan Legion itself proved most effective in bringing about the increased Romanization of the area through the efforts of its architects and engineers. Under such protection and encouragement Roman merchants must have been attracted all the more to such commercial centres as Leptis Magna, Oea, and Sabratha. The extended arm of the Roman government reached even to these places, though, and the inhabitants were subject to such regular taxes as those on the value of land and on fixed property, on income obtained from movable property, and also indirect taxes in the form of harbor dues and customs. The older local governmental system continued, however,

20

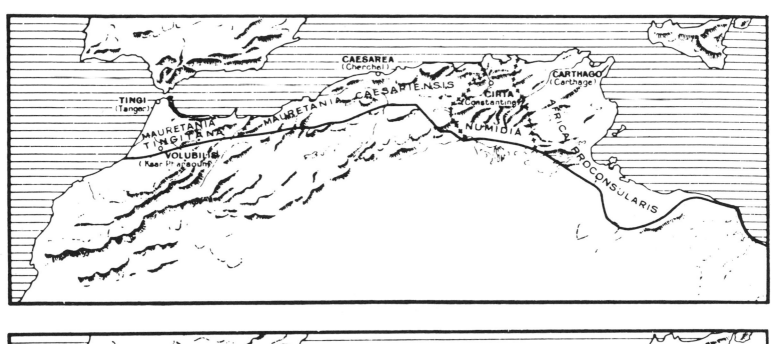

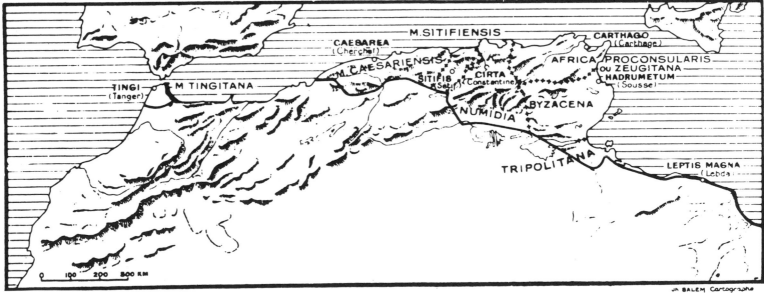

Roman Africa. *Top:* In the Severan Period. *Bottom:* After Diocletian.

and beneath the growing veneer of Roman culture there still ran a strong under-current of native Berber and Phoenician civilization. With great foresight Rome never attempted to interfere with this but wisely adapted these elements to her own purposes. Although Latin was used as the official language for the accomplishment of business by the various branches of the governor's civil and military offices, Punic was equally dominant in everyday speech and writing. Yet increasing commerce with other Mediterranean countries under the aegis of the Pax Romana brought develop-ing prosperity to the African port cities such as Utica, the new Carthage which had been reestablished, in 123 B.C., as the Colonia Karthago Iunonia, Leptis Magna, Oea, and Sabratha. Of the eastern cities Leptis Magna grew most prominently.

The peace of the coastal cities of the Emporia was not unmarred, however, for the centres of Roman culture were confined to the narrow belt of cultivable land which ran along the coast. Inland the primitive tribal people posed a continual threat. This condition of potential danger also existed further to the west, and in 17 A.D. the peace in Roman Africa was seriously disrupted by the invasion of desert tribes under the leadership of Tacfarinas, a Numidian who had finally deserted after having been trained for service as a Roman auxiliary. Incorporating into his forces at various times the native tribes of the Musulamii, the Mauri, and the Garamantes, Tacfarinas led his attacks deep into Roman territory. The Third Augustan Legion was unable to meet this invasion alone and the Ninth Hispanic Legion was transferred immediately to assist. In 24 A.D. Tacfarinas was killed and the Roman general Publius Dolabella brought the revolt to an end. With the conclusion of activities the Ninth Hispanic Legion was moved on to Pannonia and peace reigned once more in Africa.

The revolt of Tacfarinas had clearly shown, however, that it was highly imprac-tical to concentrate both military and civil authority in the hands of the proconsular governor. Consequently the emperor Gaius (37–41 A.D.) separated these two responsi-bilities, confining the realm of the governor of Africa to civil control over provincial life which was mostly concentrated in the highly developed cities of the coast. Military authority was vested in the propraetorian legate of the Third Augustan Legion, who thus in essence also assumed control over most of Numidia to the west of Africa Pro-consularis, inasmuch as this area seemed to be most in need of military observation to prevent trouble with the border tribes. The legate was stationed in the headquarters of his legion, which was for a while at Ammaedara, then Tebessa, and finally at Lam-baesis at the beginning of the second century A.D. Among his forces the legate num-bered approximately 5500 regular legionaries who were full Roman citizens, and a body of auxiliary soldiers of about the same number. These latter were enrolled from the provinces. A cohort of the regular legion was detached to serve as a guard to the governor in Carthage where there was also stationed an urban cohort sent from Rome to serve as a police force for the maintenance of peace in the city. In 42 A.D., when Mauretania was added to the Roman province as a result of the death of its king

Ptolemy at the hands of Gaius, additional auxiliary forces totaling about 15,000 men were raised for the new territory. By the middle of the second century A.D. native Africans filled not only the ranks of the auxiliary groups but also a large proportion of those in the regular legion. For the protection of the eastern parts of the province, such as the area behind Leptis Magna and Sabratha, cohorts of the legion were available for minor troubles while the entire legion could be dispatched in the event of a major uprising.

In the years following the annexation of Mauretania, Africa became rather intimately involved in affairs in Rome through such men as Aulus Vitellius, who served as proconsul of Africa under the emperor Claudius (41–54 A.D.) and later became emperor himself. Then, on the death of Nero in 68 A.D., the proconsul of Africa at the time, Clodius Macer, turned his own rebellion into a serious threat to seize the throne. In setting himself up as a candidate Macer attempted to supplement the Third Augustan Legion by raising an extra force, the First Macrianan Legion, so as to provide stronger military backing for his project. The emperor Galba disbanded this legion when he came to the throne in 68 A.D., but the emperor Vitellius reconstituted it again in the following year. Upon the latter's death in December of the same year the legion finally disappeared completely from the records.

Although Nero had paid small attention to the military aspects of his administration the serious confusion brought on by the various army units at the time of his death indicated to the emperor Vespasian and several of his successors that a close intimacy with the army had to be maintained. This policy was an important facet of the reigns of Trajan and also Hadrian who, in the year 128 A.D., landed at Carthage and traveled inland to Lambaesis where the Third Augustan Legion was then quartered. At the camp he personally reviewed the troops in special maneuvers and by this touch strengthened the devotion of the forces upon whose loyalty the safety of Roman Africa depended. Nor was this purely unselfish attention on the part of the emperor, for by this time the entire province of Africa was supplying enough grain to meet the needs of Rome for perhaps eight months of the year. Oil ranked next in importance as an article of wholesale export and therein lay the importance of Leptis Magna. Through this port passed huge quantities of oil pressed from olives grown in the orchards which covered the Tarhuna plateau to the southwest of the city. For the increasing prosperity of this region protection had to be guaranteed against the Garamantes, a native tribe on the fringes of the desert to the south. From other parts of the province came fine purple dye, figs, truffles, cucumbers, expensive woods and marbles, animals for use in the amphitheatres, and numerous medicinal items. The second century A.D. saw Roman civilization in Africa flourishing with increasing lustre, encouraged by the ever-growing demands of Italy. In addition the province had attracted Italian land investors who developed some fairly large estates which were frequently leased out to *coloni* for cultivation. Although originally free tenants, these *coloni* gradually became bound not only for their responsibility in returning a certain percentage of crops to the government but also by the obligation to work on domain land. Much private territory in the province had come into the imperial domain by confiscation under Nero and this too was parceled out and sublet for cultivation. During the second century A.D. these business interests led to an increase in the economic and social activities of the province, which found expression in typical Roman building ventures.

Prosperity for many sections of Africa Proconsularis reached its culminating glory in the early third century A.D. under the encouragement of the Severan emperors. When Septimius Severus ascended the imperial throne in 193 A.D., pride of a new sort swelled up in the breasts of the citizens of Africa, for Septimius himself had been born in Leptis Magna. Nor did he forget the country of his birth. Concern for his native land led Septimius to reassess the military measures taken to protect the province against incursions of native tribes from the interior. Heretofore the Roman military policy appears to have been one of merely depending upon units of the Third Augustan Legion which could be sent into the interior to subdue and punish any native uprisings. In this manner was protection given to the narrow civilized coastal belt which included Oea, Sabratha, and Leptis Magna. While such military units probably were quartered from time to time in these three cities and occasionally in villages along the road which ran parallel to the coast atop the Gebel escarpment, they were not garrison troops located in highly organized Roman fortifications. With Septimius' restudy of this situation a new scheme developed. This involved the creation of a deep protective area of civilized native agricultural settlement in the hinterland south and southeast of Leptis Magna, including the Wadi Sofeggin and running down to the region of the Wadi Zemzem. To lend further strength to this plan, several military stations or fortifications were erected on the road leading southeast into the Upper Sofeggin area from the vicinity of Zintan on the Gebel road. Under Septimius a part of the Third Augustan Legion was stationed at Ain Wif (ancient Thenadassa) on this same road which ran up from Leptis Magna through Medina Doga (ancient Mesphe) and on westward to Turris Tamalleni in modern Tunisia. While in the earlier period of the empire this road may have served as a form of *limes* or border limit, it was then never a chain of connected military settlements. Indeed, at the time of its original demarcation during the reign of Tiberius (14–37 A.D.) it could not have been any more military than commercial in nature, since it only reached at first from Leptis Magna to Mesphe, a distance of forty-two miles. Under Septimius Severus, however, the road passed all the way from Turris Tamalleni along the Gebel range to Leptis Magna and formed a stable military and commercial inner frontier connection for the developing agricultural settlements in the Sofeggin region. Protection here was also guaranteed by outposts of the Third Augustan Legion stationed on the desert fringes to the south at Bu-Ngem, Gheria el-Garbia, and Ghadames. Throughout the reigns of Septimius' successors Caracalla and Alexander Severus this protective zone behind the

24

coastal cities of Leptis Magna, Oea, and Sabratha was further developed by the construction of fortified farms in the wheat growing area of the Sofeggin. It was Alexander Severus who supplemented the fortifications on the desert border by establishing the fort at Gheria el-Garbia already mentioned. When the Third Augustan Legion was finally disbanded in 238 A.D. the responsibility of maintaining the *Limes Tripolitanus* devolved upon the agricultural landholders dwelling on their estates in towerlike buildings surrounded by ditches. These men were of Libyan-Phoenician background and in many instances had served as auxiliaries in the Roman legion; on being mustered out, they had received grants of land in the *limes* region with the understanding that they stand ready to provide military service in their area when the necessity arose. After 238 A.D. forces of native border troops termed *limitanei* were organized by zonal divisions, each division being placed in the charge of an officer known as the *praepositus*. The *Limes Tentheitanus* was one of these zones on the border between Tripolitania and Numidia and had some of its forces stationed at Gasr Duib on the road leading from the main Gebel road down toward Mizda in the Upper Sofeggin. Several additional defensive sites have been recognized along the Wadi Sofeggin and the Wadi Zemzem.

To the east of Bu-Ngem and Sirte (ancient Maccomades) Roman penetration was confined to the coast and reached eastward to Cyrenaica. Very little is known of military protective measures in this region. To the west of Tripolitania, however, evidence indicates that, at least in part, the *limes* in Tunisia was comprised of the more standard *fosse,* or ditch, often accompanied by a wall of earth. Such a *fosse* was constructed by Scipio to delimit Rome's first holdings in Africa. In the first century A.D. Roman civilization moved further inland and military structures were erected at such sites as Ammaedara, Lambaesis, and even the advanced post at Gemellae which was founded by Hadrian.

Although Septimius Severus showered many favors upon the cities of his homeland, the very steps which he took for the protection of Tripolitania probably served eventually to weaken Roman domination in this section of the African coast. With the end of the Severan dynasty in 235 A.D. invasions and civil war disrupted the Roman world and Tripolitania fell subject to the general decline in the west. The creation of self-subsistent native strongholds in the interior, combining an agricultural existence with native military preparedness, only served to encourage the growth of a feeling of independence.

When Diocletian came to the throne in 284 A.D. the situation throughout the entire empire had so changed as to require a completely new approach to imperial administration. Africa drew its share of attention and fell subject to the general imperial policy of subdivision. By 293 A.D. Mauretania Sitifensis had been created while Byzacena, formed from the southern part of Africa Proconsularis, appeared shortly after 294. Africa Proconsularis itself was enlarged through the addition of a part of

Numidia, and for the first time Tripolitana appears as a separate province sometime between 294 and 307. Whereas the coast of Tripolitana had earlier been controlled by a legate of the proconsul of Africa and the interior by the legate of the Third Augustan Legion, now it had its own governor bearing the title of *praeses*. All four of these provinces formed the diocese of North Africa, which was administered by a vicar. North Africa in turn belonged in the praefecture of Italy ruled by one of the four praetorian praefects.

Although the governor of a province was primarily a judicial official, he also bore the responsibility of administering the tax levy and enforcing the fulfillment of liturgies or public burdens assigned to the various members of the local curia as well as the *navicularii* or groups of men owning commercial sailing vessels. The vicars of the dioceses were directly responsible to the emperor, and in the case of Africa the vicar assumed the special burden of assuring the collection of grain and oil supplies for Rome. This obligation of supplying Rome with grain and oil was termed the *annona*. At first the responsibility of collecting it rested with the governor at Carthage, who delegated the charge to local officials and members of the curia. In the time of Diocletian the proconsul of Africa Proconsularis directed this in his own domain while the vicar of the diocese of Africa assumed its direction in the other African provinces. From 395 A.D., however, the vicar of Africa held this responsibility in Africa Proconsularis as well. The portion of wheat or oil to be paid by landowners was delivered three times a year to the municipal granaries, the *horrea,* which were managed by officials called *praepositi horreorum.* When the collections were complete the *vir clarissimus praefectus annonae Africae* then took charge of transporting it to Rome and thus fulfilled the obligations for the *annona* which rested directly upon the praetorian praefect. The *praefectus annonae* was assisted in this transportation problem by the *navicularii,* merchants who possessed the means of shipping the wheat and oil across the Mediterranean to Italy.

This highly developed chain of responsibility for guaranteeing free grain and oil to the populace of Rome was completely dependent upon peace in the agricultural areas of Africa. Most Roman emperors were only too well aware of the dangerous revolts which could occur in the capital of Rome if anything should prevent the arrival of ships bearing the promised dole. When Diocletian reviewed the military situation in Africa he found that, in spite of the emperor Gaius' attempt to separate the civil from the military offices, the disbanding of the Third Augustan Legion in 238 A.D. had permitted the provincial governors again to secure command of the armed forces in their provinces. During the latter part of the third century A.D. it had become the practice to appoint a special commander or *dux* to carry on especially important military campaigns. This, however, was too casual a system for Diocletian and he proceeded to reform the military organization into two units. One was a central mobile force and the other an appropriate number of squadrons to be permanently stationed on the frontiers. During the reign of Constantine the position of *comes* was created for the commander of the army of Africa. In Tripolitana, however, the local governor still controlled the local forces, probably only *limitanei*, and in this capacity employed the title *dux* through most of the fourth century. During this same century it is interesting to note that in an army of 21,000 men in Africa, 9500 of these were mounted horsemen. This clearly shows the value which the Roman command placed on cavalry in this region.

Although revolts did occur among native African tribes during the early years of the reign of Diocletian and Maximian, the next serious threat to Tripolitana appeared in 363 A.D. when the Austuriani, a tribe to the southeast of Tripolitana, invaded that province and penetrated as far as the very walls of Leptis Magna. Entreaties for help sent to the *comes Africae,* or Roman commander in Africa, Romanus, accomplished little, and in the succeeding years Tripolitana was invaded again and the land around Leptis ravaged once more, while in 365 A.D. Sabratha was partially destroyed. Direct appeals to the emperor Valentinian I failed, and it would appear that similar raids continued into the beginning of the fifth century. All of these raids seem to have been carried out by tribes who swarmed through the very areas in the Wadi Zemzem and the Wadi Sofeggin where earlier imperial policy had developed native fortified dwellings to serve as protection against just such attacks. One wonders just how this was possible if the inhabitants of these regions were truly faithful in the performance of their duties. On the other hand, the incursions may have come by way of the Tarhuna plateau directly south of Leptis and Oea. An inscription found in this region and evidently dating to the end of the fourth century or the beginning of the fifth records the gratefulness of a family saved from destruction at the hands perhaps of the very natives who attacked the coastal towns.

In other parts of Africa, from 372 to 374 A.D., native uprisings led by Firmus, a native chieftain, proved so threatening in Mauretania Sitifensis and Mauretania Caesariensis that the emperor himself at last observed the incapabilities of the same Romanus, *comes Africae.* The imperial *magister equitum* Theodosius was dispatched to quell the revolt. In 397 A.D. Gildo, a brother of Firmus, transferred his allegiance as *comes Africae* from Honorius to Arcadius, the eastern Roman emperor at Constantinople. Stilicho, sent by Honorius to recover Africa and preserve the all-important source of grain supply for Rome, defeated Gildo in 398 and the office of *comes Africae* was given to Stilicho's brother-in-law Bathanarius.

Life in Roman Africa had now become quite disturbed by internal complications as well as those brought about by tribal threats on the borders. From the great days of Septimius Severus Africa had begun its decline, perhaps slower than throughout other parts of the western empire but nonetheless certain. Increasing bondage to civic obligations involving more burdensome financial outlays undermined the social fibre of the provinces. Most directly affected by these government policies were the promi-

27

nent citizens who comprised the *curia* or local senate. One of their greatest problems was the collection of taxes. Any unfavorable difference between the assessed tax and that actually collected had to be made up by these *curiales* or members of the *curia*. But this was only the greatest of their many grievances. During the fourth century many emperors tried to relieve the situation, but by the end of the century affairs had returned to their former state. Rapacity on the part of government officials in the provinces was always one of the problems of Roman imperial administration. This evil, often activated through connivance with influential officers at court, added more to the burden of the provincials during the third and fourth centuries A.D. The great building surge in Africa during the reign of Septimius Severus appears to have exhausted the financial resources of such a town as Leptis Magna, and in other towns the financial status must have been severely threatened. Even though subsequent imperial patronage encouraged new building efforts, these were largely concentrated in Africa Proconsularis and Numidia. Local initiative and civic pride in the cities of Tripolitana and much of Roman Africa continued in decline under the increasing pressure and limitation of movement placed on the *curiales* and other members of the local societal structure.

There was other unrest in Africa during the fourth century, though, and this came as a direct result of the Christian persecutions under Diocletian. Throughout the early empire the Christian Church had survived the sporadic persecutions of the second and third centuries, gaining ever more additional strength. When Diocletian published his first edict against the Church in 303 A.D. he instituted a program of persecution which varied widely in intensity during the year immediately following. In the east the Caesar Galerius put the program into force with pagan devotion. In the west Constantius instrumented the drive in his praefecture of Gaul and Britain with very weak purpose, while Maximian, on the other hand, executed the edict with a strong hand in Africa as well as in the other dioceses under his control. After the retirement of Diocletian and Maximian the new rulers in the west, Constantine and Maxentius, desisted from this program and eventually granted toleration to the Christians in their domains. With the coming of peace in Africa, however, a more insidious threat arose in the body of the Church. How was the Church to deal with members and even officials who had capitulated to the government and had surrendered the scriptures for destruction? In 313 A.D. Anullinus, the proconsul of Africa, informed the emperor Constantine of this newly developed schism wherein the leaders of the Church in Numidia contested the recent election of Caecilian to the position of Bishop of Carthage, which city had become the ecclesiastical capital of Africa. The charge, later proven false, was that Caecilian had been ordained by a *traditor,* one who had been guilty of refusing to protect the prerogatives and possessions of the Church during the great persecution. A rival bishop was elected and the contest became so disruptive to the peace of the provinces that imperial intervention was necessary. By

28

the time Constantine summoned a council in October 313 to decide the contest, Majorinus the rival bishop had died, and had been replaced by Donatus, whose name now became attached to the new religious movement. When the Donatists refused to accept the decision of the Council of Rome in favor of Caecilian the emperor summoned another council at Arles in 314. In 316 Constantine declared his decision to uphold the rights of Caecilian. The subsequent actions of the Donatists led him to attempt to coerce them in 321, but after only a few months this policy was brought to an end. Throughout the fourth century the Donatists fomented more trouble, mostly centered in Numidia where they were strongest. Mauretania Sitifensis also felt their disturbing influence. The revolts of Firmus and Gildo in the latter half of the century found some encouragement among the Donatists, although Gildo himself had good reason to complain of their lack of support. Even more discredit was attached to the Donatist movement through the brigandage of bands of wandering agricultural workers of the poorest class. These were called *circumcelliones*. Various attempts to repress this schismatic body in the African Church were made during the fourth century, and occasional encouragement came to them from such as the emperor Julian and the *comes Africae* Gildo. At last in 403, however, a Donatist bishop was declared a heretic by the proconsul of Africa and an imperial edict of February 12, 405, proclaimed Donatism a heresy. Until now able to sustain itself within the frame-work of the law, Donatism, stigmatized with the label of heresy, was severely weakened. The final blow came with the condemnation of Donatism in 411 at the Conference of Carthage. The laws promulgated at the conclusion of this conference accomplished the end of the Donatist heresy to all intents and purposes, though some isolated Donatist bodies continued in existence for several more centuries.

Hardly had the imperial government committed itself to the extermination of the Donatist heresy when it was confronted with another serious situation in the African provinces. Indications of weakness in the imperial succession in Rome led to increasing discontent and difficulty in the provincial administration. With the death of the Vandal Stilicho and the termination of Bathanarius' tenure in Africa the position of *comes Africae* passed to Heraclian, who aspired to great authority in court circles as a highly influential general. At first loyal to the emperor Honorius during the Gothic threats of Alaric and Attalus, Heraclian finally revolted in 413 A.D. and attempted to invade Italy. Mustering his African army, he called upon the great African grain fleet to transport the forces overseas to Italy. Once on land there, however, Heraclian was defeated and finally executed.

When Honorius died in 423 the western empire of Rome passed on to his nephew Valentinian III, who was guided during the early years of his reign by Galla Placidia, the sister of Honorius. It was unfortunate for the young emperor that misunderstandings arose between the empress Placidia and the *comes Africae* Boniface. The latter's attitude toward Rome became so hostile that in 427 two successive military ventures

29

became necessary to subdue Boniface. In this state of affairs Africa offered itself as a tempting lure to the Asding Vandals who had moved into the southern area of Spain in 419. Encouraged by Boniface's hostility toward the Roman court, and not necessarily directly invited by Boniface as later historians suggested, this body of Vandals along with a small group of Alans crossed into Africa in May 429. Probably by February of this same year Boniface had become reconciled with the imperial government and the expedition of the Vandals was regarded as a true invasion for the purpose of securing new territory. In Spain the Vandals had eventually been recognized as *foederati* or allies of the Roman government, and their progress through western Africa was so irresistible that in 435 Rome was compelled to recognize them as *foederati* now in Africa. In February of this year a treaty was signed with the Vandals, probably at Hippo, establishing them as *foederati* in proconsular Numidia with Hippo as their capital.

The peace was short-lived, however, and in 439 Gaiseric, who had led them into Africa from Spain, conducted a successful Vandal attack on Carthage. The years of the reign of Gaiseric who died in 477 were dated from this event. By 442 the Roman government was no longer able to maintain the fallacy that the Vandals were merely residents on Roman territory, and in this year Valentinian concluded a treaty with Gaiseric whereby north Africa was divided between the Vandals and the Romans.

This was the birth of the Vandal state, consisting of a specified geographical area over which it exerted complete authority. By the treaty the Vandals gained Africa Proconsularis, Byzacena, the eastern and larger portion of Numidia including its southern borders, and finally the territories of the Gaetulia and the Abaritana. The latter group of people are connected with the western section of Tripolitana, which thus came under the influence of Gaiseric. Indeed, other evidence suggests that before 455 Gaiseric exercised his authority along the coast of Tripolitana at least as far as Oea, thus including Sabratha in his realm as well.

For themselves the Romans retained Mauretania Caesariensis, Mauretania Sitifensis, a section of Numidia including the city of Cirta, and also perhaps the eastern section of Tripolitana. By 455 Gaiseric had become so strong as to invade Italy, capture Rome, and carry off as hostages Valentinian's widow Eudoxia and her two daughters Eudoxia and Placidia.

Shortly after his accession to the throne of the eastern Roman empire in 474, Zeno sent the patrician Severus to Carthage to negotiate a peace agreement with Gaiseric. This was a most appropriate move on Zeno's part, inasmuch as his predecessor Leo had dispatched a great army on 1100 ships, at a cost of 130,000 livres of gold, under the generalship of Basiliscus, the empress' brother, to defeat the Vandals in 468. The expedition had failed miserably and the more successful march of Byzantine soldiers under Heraclius through Tripolitana toward Carthage also had come to nothing. Thus, by his treaty, Zeno recognized an accomplished fact and the Vandals

30

were left with their African domains as well as Sicily, Sardinia, Corsica, and the Balearic Islands. Once again the wealthy cities of Tripolitana found themselves under Vandal rule.

Other than establishing an elaborate Vandal court at Carthage with offices strongly resembling some of those in the Roman imperial court, the Vandals appear to have allowed local government to continue much in the old manner. The old system established for the administration of justice continued in force excepting for matters concerning major religious problems. This was understandable in view of the fact that, as Arians, the Vandals were interested in increasing the authority of their Church at the expense of the African Catholic Church. In customs the Vandals were all too anxious to adopt the luxurious ways of the Romans, and Latin continued as the predominating tongue, thus making bilinguists of many Vandals.

When Justinian ascended the imperial throne in Constantinople in 527 A.D., the policy of the Roman government assumed new vigor. Determined to reestablish Roman prestige in north Africa Justinian appointed his most capable general, Belisarius, to the command of a Byzantine army which set sail from Constantinople in the summer of 533. By September Carthage had fallen, and in December the Vandal king Gelimer was taken captive, thus bringing to an end the great Vandal kingdom.

In 534 the reconquered provinces of Tripolitana, Byzacena, Africa Proconsularis, Numidia and Mauretania Sitifensis were placed under the charge of the patrician Solomon, who united civil and military authority under the titles of *praetorian praefect* and *magister militum* of Africa. Difficulties in restoring peace among the various native groups increased to such an extent that Solomon was replaced by Justinian's own nephew Germanus in 538. Germanus was successful in quelling these disturbances, and in 539 Solomon was reinstated to complete the pacification of the country, and ruled until his death in 544. On this occasion local uprisings again broke out in the Berber areas, but the general John Troglita finally combated them so successfully that these Roman provinces remained peaceful throughout the rest of their existence under Byzantine control.

Mauretania Caesariensis and Mauretania Tingitana had not been regained by the Byzantine forces, and these were held within the empire only by the most broadly interpreted bonds of association. Indeed, under Diocletian, Tingitana had been separated from the African sphere of influence by being incorporated into the province of Spain. Civil and military authority in the Byzantine provinces of Africa were divided, although in cases of emergency both could be combined into one office. At the head of the civil branch was the *praetorian praefect,* who governed the praefecture of Africa, which included the five provinces already mentioned as well as Sardinia and Corsica. Beneath the praefect were seven governors titled either *consulares* or *praesides.* Governors with the rank of *consularis* ruled Zeugitana (old Africa Proconsularis), Byzacena, and Tripolitana, while Sardinia, Numidia, Mauretania Sitifensis, and a sector of the reincorporated Mauretania Caesariensis were governed by men with the rank of *praeses*.

The military command in Africa was placed in the charge of a *magister militum* who directed the over-all administration of the four military districts in the praefecture (Tripolitana, Byzacena, Numidia, and Mauretania). Each district was controlled by a *dux* who supervised the *limitanei* and whatever forces were put in charge of tribunes. The *limitanei* were a continuation of the pre-Vandal Roman border protective pattern. Each was granted a section of land on which to sustain himself and his family, but this land could be held and even inherited only on the condition that the owner provide military service in his area when the need arose.

Inasmuch as the Vandals had destroyed the protective walls of many towns in Africa Justinian found it necessary to rebuild these, although in most cases the area enclosed was much smaller than in former times. In addition numerous Byzantine forts were constructed as far west as the straits of Gibraltar. Beyond these protective measures, special alliances were formed with the leaders of various border tribes, thus establishing a series of barbarian client princes called *Mauri pacifici*. The general pattern of refortification in Africa, however, clearly indicated a Byzantine withdrawal inwards from the earlier imperial limits.

The recurrence of numerous minor wars in Africa by the end of the sixth century led to the creation of a new form of governorship called the *exarchate*, which now permanently combined both civil and military powers. This official was of extremely high political and social rank and exerted almost unlimited powers. This same period also found the imperial government restudying the provincial border limits in Africa, as a result of which Mauretania Sitifensis and Mauretania Caesariensis were combined to form the new province of Mauretania Prima; the area further to the west, Septum, was added to the Byzantine holdings in southern Spain to become Mauretania Secunda. Tripolitana itself, probably during the reign of the emperor Maurice (582–602 A.D.), was separated from Africa and joined to the province of Egypt.

The Byzantine reorganization meant little to the dying culture in north Africa, which had become thoroughly exhausted and depopulated by the wars of the sixth century. Depredations of undisciplined soldiers contributed to the weakened condition, and the territory proved only too fertile for the Moslem conquerors who, first establishing an outpost at Al-Qayrawan, were finally able to seize Carthage in 698.

2

THE TOWN OF LEPTIS MAGNA

FROM THE GULF OF GABES in southeastern Tunisia the sandy beaches of modern Tripolitania stretch eastward to Cyrenaica, offering six hundred and sixty miles of low, unprotected sea-front. In the early years of the first millennium B.C. this offered little welcome to the Phoenician merchants who plied the waters of the Mediterranean. For those more venturesome among them who sought and found the protective harbors at Oea (Tripoli) and Leptis Magna, great promise was extended in the form of trade with natives of the interior. From their oasis homes in the deserts of the Fezzan the primitive tribes sent caravans bearing precious and fascinating items of trade up through the plateau ranges and then down into the coastal plain of the Gefara and across to the coastal trading posts, where they could be exchanged with the Phoenician merchants. Recognizing this commercial potential these merchants from the eastern Mediterranean established regular ports of call along the Tripolitanian coast. Among these was the little settlement at the mouth of the Wadi Lebda later known as Leptis Magna which, like its sister establishments of Oea and Sabratha to the west, probably owed its early growth to these trans-Saharan caravans. Unlike these other two sites, however, Leptis was not separated from the hinterland by the Gefara plain. Instead the curving mountainous range of the Gebel swung northward to approach the coast directly behind Leptis. Here it diminished to the limestone Tarhuna plateau, overlaid with a rich stratum of soil. During the period of its development under Carthage and then republican Rome, Leptis spread its influence back up into these coastal highlands.

It was here that the cultivation of olive trees was so successful as to make Leptis one of the largest centres in Africa for the production of olive oil. To the southeast of the Tarhuna plateau a series of wadis, such as the Wadi Sofeggin and the Wadi Zemzem, run northeastward to the coast. Although there was much less rainfall in these semidesert areas, settlements along the sides of the wadis gradually converted this section into an important wheat-producing region. Thus Leptis Magna became a town whose prosperity depended far more on the agricultural produce of its inland holdings than on any caravan trade across the Sahara. Nevertheless such caravans still came northward from the regions of the Niger and Lake Chad with precious goods strapped tightly to the lumbering camels, animals which perhaps were introduced to this part of north Africa during the Ptolemaic or early Roman period. Although Roman forces occasionally penetrated to the northern edges of the desert, the Romans were generally content to leave the caravan trade to such desert tribes as the Garamantes.

33

The growing preponderance of agricultural items, and particularly of olive oil, in the markets of Leptis Magna is clearly indicated in the assessment of 3 million pounds (1,067,800 litres) of oil for which the city was made responsible by Julius Caesar. During the reign of Augustus the increase of wealth as well as population made imminent a reassessment of the town's physical appearance. New dwellings and public structures had sprung up along the road leading inland from the original Phoenician settlement near the promontory defining the northwestern side of the harbor at the mouth of the Wadi Lebda. Restricted on the east by this same wadi, the expanding town had grown toward the west from the road. In the northwest sector the civic-minded citizens of Leptis constructed a Forum, now identified as the Forum Vetus to differentiate it from the later Forum of Severan times. On its northwestern side the Forum Vetus was originally dominated by the Temple of Liber Pater, who was equated with the god Bacchus. Both he and Hercules were worshiped as the patron deities of Leptis Magna. The temple was erected atop a podium which was divided internally into a series of crypts surrounding a solid core. A row of chambers or *tabernae* evidently stood against the north face of the podium. The solid core of the podium's interior supported the *cella* or central temple chamber above. In standard fashion a colonnade surrounded this *cella* on both sides and across the front, where a flight of steps led up to the top of the podium.

During the reign of Augustus, when the Temple of Liber Pater was built, another temple, smaller and dedicated to a deity not yet identified, was installed a distance to the northeast of the larger temple. In the Augustan paving of the Forum in front of this temple an inscription was placed bearing the name of Cnaeus Calpurnius Piso, who thus may be associated with the building.

At some period between 14 and 19 A.D. the cult of Rome and Augustus was honored with a fine temple set up between that of Liber Pater and the smaller temple of unknown dedication to the northeast. It is known from inscriptions that at least as early as 8 B.C. this cult had been introduced to Leptis, for in that year the two citizens Iddibale and Ammicar were officiating as its priests (*flamines Augusti*). The erection of a new temple in the period immediately following the death of Augustus in 14 A.D. was a most appropriate method of indicating devotion to the memory of the great emperor. The temple itself, which stood upon a podium, was constructed entirely of local limestone, with a *cella* surrounded on the sides and front by a colonnade with column capitals in the Ionic style. Probably during the reign of Claudius (41–54 A.D.) when new paving was laid in the Forum the podium of the Temple of Rome and Augustus was extended forward so as to form a rostrum for public addresses. A flight of steps on each side led to the top of the platform.

The entire southeastern end of the Forum was bounded by the side wall of the old basilica or Basilica Vetus. With the axis running in a northeast-southwest line, this building was also built entirely of the local limestone and so probably dated to the first century A.D. In design it consisted of a rectangular hall with two entrance doors at the northeast end. On the interior a colonnade ran around all four sides, and against the southwest end wall three exedrae of rectangular form were built for the seats of the judges or officials presiding over law cases.

During the reign of Augustus the town of Leptis Magna had already achieved a respectable degree of prosperity and importance and under increasing pressure from the population it expanded to the southwest of the Forum Vetus. In this area a Market was laid out, surrounded by a perimeter wall of sandstone blocks resting on a ground course of limestone, and in characteristic Roman style was completely outfitted with accommodations for the sale of foods. In the Augustan period the west wall of the enclosure had a central entrance doorway flanked by two smaller entrances. On the exterior surface of this wall an inscription in Latin records the munificence of Anno-bal Rufus, who financed the construction of the entire Market in 9–8 B.C. In a later rebuilding these entrances were altered to provide larger doorways to the interior and the sandstone wall with its stucco covering was plastered over. The exterior was then decorated with incised circles and a painted guilloche border, while the interior surface of the wall was ornamented with a narrow frieze of cupids and garlands. The court within the Market walls was surrounded with a colonnade of black granite Corinthian columns and in the centre of the enclosure stood two octagonal porticos, each with a circular structure in the middle. Sales counters were placed between the columns of these porticos for the display of edibles to be purchased by the town's citizens. One of these buildings or *tholoi* contained an inscription giving the name of the person responsible for its construction. This again was Annobal Rufus. At the southeastern end of the Market another entrance provided access from the *Cardo* or main north-south street (Plates 3 and 4). Spanning this street, just southwest of the entrance to the Market, an unassuming single arch was dedicated to the emperor Tiberius in 35–36 A.D. (Plate 25).

The generosity of Annobal Rufus had not yet attained its full expression, however, and before the Market was finished he must have been thinking already of another typically Roman structure which the citizens of Leptis sorely needed. Finally, in 1–2 A.D., this too was accomplished, and a beautiful theatre stood revealed just to the west of the Market. Designed in the standard semicircular form used by the Romans, the orchestra and the lower rows of the *cavea* or seating area of the auditorium were excavated from the virgin rock of the site. The most important seating area at the front was separated from the rest of the seats by a low marble screen, while the lower half of the rest of the auditorium was divided into six radial sections by flights of steps running down from the five entrances installed halfway up the expanse of seats (Plates 7, 8, and 16). Six other flights of steps starting at the centre top of the lower sections led on up to the top of the auditorium, where a semicircular colonnaded walk ran around the upper edge of the supporting wall. In the middle of this colon-

35

nade, opposite the centre of the stage, was set a small Temple of Ceres (Plates, 9, 10, 11, and 12). The uppermost rows of seats were supported on great piers of stone and concrete, and are now largely nonexistent.

The outer wall of the auditorium, which concealed the corridors and stairs leading to the upper seating sections, was completely unpretentious in its decoration, having only simple moldings and pilasters with five arched openings leading to the corridors inside. Between the auditorium and the stage an entrance corridor on each side permitted unencumbered access to the seating arrangements for the notables (Plate 16).

The stage was probably made of wooden sections resting in front upon a stone wall ornamented with niches displaying a variety of classical statues (Plate 19). At the back of the stage rose the great stone ornamental back-drop or *scaenae frons*. This was arranged in the form of three apses with a fine portico of columns, one row superimposed upon the other, following the contour of the wall (Plates 17, 18, 19, 20, and 21). To the sides of the stage retiring rooms were provided and, on the southeast, a room or court over the entrance to which was placed the inscription identifying the donor of the Theatre as Annobal Rufus (Plates 5 and 6). Behind the stage a portico was arranged around an irregularly shaped court in which stood a temple dedicated to the deified emperors. This certainly must have been connected with the Theatre, since it was the classical tradition to have such a portico for the protection of patrons in inclement weather or for little promenades between theatrical presentations.

Another citizen, Iddibal Caphada Aemilius, perhaps encouraged by the example of Annobal Rufus, turned his resources to the construction of a Chalcidicum (possibly a market for dry-goods) to the southeast of the Theatre. Opening onto the *Cardo* which issued in a southwesterly direction from the southwest side of the Forum Vetus, the Chalcidicum consisted of a portico of Corinthian columns surmounting a broad flight of steps (Plate 22). In the centre of a row of shops ranged behind the portico stood a small temple and behind these, perhaps also a part of the Chalcidicum, lay a large rectangular space open to the sky and surrounded by porticos (Plate 24). An inscription from the architrave of the main portico of the Chalcidicum, facing on the street, indicates that the already-mentioned Iddibal Caphada Aemilius erected the building in 11–12 A.D. (Plate 23). At a later date this main portico evidently was altered and cisterns were added to it, one at either end. Within the rectangular area behind the shops the southwestern portico with its double row of columns was incorporated into a long water tank also at a late period (Plates 15 and 16).

The great building activity in which Leptis thus engaged at the beginning of the imperial period was symbolic of the wealth which accrued to her from her hold over the interior agricultural regions.

To facilitate movement from the city into the Tarhuna section, a road was laid out by the proconsul of Africa Lucius Aelius Lamia, holding office during the reign

36

of Tiberius (14–37 A.D.), and this led up into the plateau for a distance of forty-two miles to the site of Mesphe. Although perhaps originally conceived to permit more rapid military movement in dealing with tribes of the interior, this road undoubtedly facilitated the transportation of produce down to the seaport. An inscription on the previously-mentioned Arch of Tiberius also indicates that movement of traffic within the city was somewhat improved at this time by the repaving of some city streets. Communication along the coast was already established by a road which ran westward from Leptis through Oea (Tripoli) and Sabratha and on to Tacapae.

While these provisions were all accomplished under Roman rule, one must not consider Leptis Magna and its surrounding territory as being largely populated by Roman colonists or Roman citizens. Quite to the contrary, the inhabitants were largely natives of Punic or Lybian background, and a strong Punic element persisted beneath the superficial veneer of Roman culture. Leptis even minted its own coinage with Punic legends until the reign of Tiberius, and neo-Punic inscriptions occur during the first century A.D., parallel with those in Latin. Indeed, aside from Romans stationed in Africa as government officials, actual Romans or Italians on the scene were very scarce and appear to have been there only to develop or protect some commercial or agricultural interest.

During the reign of Augustus, Leptis Magna was classified as a *civitas libera et immunis,* or a free community, over which the governor had an absolute minimum of control. As such Leptis retained its two *suphetes* at the head of its government, with the *mhzm,* similar to the Roman *aediles,* as minor magistrates. In addition there were such sacred officials as the *'addir 'ararim* or *praefectus sacrorum,* the *nēquīm ēlim,* and probably a sacred college of fifteen members. These offices were still in effective operation when Leptis was made a *municipium* with a certain degree of Roman rights and privileges at some time between 61 and 68 A.D., during the rule of Nero.

When the citizens first began to enjoy the fine colonnaded porticos erected in the Forum Vetus on three of its sides, in the year 53 A.D., they probably had little thought for the troubles which might befall them from tribes of the inland deserts. It is true that such danger was always present and never to be ignored. For this reason the citizens certainly must by this time have had some form of city wall or protective construction surrounding their city.

In preparing the harbor for the increased commercial activity which had already stirred the city into new life, the engineers studied the problem of the Wadi Lebda, whose waters could rush down in torrents without warning and devastate the harbor constructions as well as any civic buildings along the wadi. As a result of this examination the water of the Wadi Lebda was blocked by a dam and detoured through a new channel cut to the south of the city. This led the stream across to the western channel of the Wadi er-Rsaf, which conducted it to the sea. In excavating this channel large mounds of earth were thrown up, now called the *Monticelli.* It is possible that these were also conceived as a defensive wall, standing either by themselves or as advanced works guarding a more substantial wall closer to the buildings grouped near the civic centres.

In any event, Leptis was suddenly called on, in the year 69 A.D., to turn all of her defensive arrangements to good advantage. Trouble came from a rather unexpected source, the city of Oea to the west. Rivalry between the two cities at first developed into a series of minor raids for the purpose of stealing grain and cattle. Then pitched battles ensued, in which Oea, being the weaker of the two cities, determined to secure outside assistance. For her allies she turned to the Garamantes, a native tribe of the interior, who immediately invaded the lands around Leptis Magna and confined the terrified citizens to the area within the city walls. Relief came soon, however, when the Roman forces under the command of Valerius Festus arrived on the scene. Most of the booty seized by the Garamantes was recovered and returned to the people of Leptis, who once more resumed their daily activities undisturbed.

Not too long after this event the Forum Vetus was graced, at its southern angle, with a Temple of Magna Mater, dedicated in 72 A.D., and a Flavian arch set up over the *Cardo,* probably on the site of the later sixth-century Byzantine gate. On the southwest side of the Forum Vetus, at its northwest end, another temple of unknown dedication was built some time near the end of this first century A.D. By this period the conservatism of the local Punic aristocracy seems to have weakened to the point of developing a fairly typical Roman civic life and this is clearly shown by the fact that in the reign of Domitian (81–96 A.D.) many prominent families in Leptis had come to hold Roman citizenship.

By the time of Trajan's accession to the throne of the empire in 98 the impressive accomplishments and undeniable importance of Leptis Magna demanded a reconsideration of the city's status in the organization of the empire. Trajan, during the few years intervening between the second Dacian war (105–106 A.D.) and his departure in 113 for his eastern campaigns, devoted his attention to the administrative problems of his empire. As a result he soon recognized the increased importance of Leptis by raising it to the rank of a Roman colony bearing the title *Colonia Ulpia Traiana Leptis.* The new status meant that the old Punic system of local government was to be replaced with one headed by two *duoviri,* having a hierarchy of officials bearing the regular Roman titles. The inhabitants themselves were now considered Roman citizens with most of the attendant privileges.

Perhaps as a symbol of the great recognition bestowed upon the town by the emperor a tastefully designed four-sided arch was erected in limestone over the intersection of two streets at the northeast corner of the Chalcidicum. Dedicated to Trajan, this was constructed by the legate Lucius Asinius Rufus, possibly through the direction of the proconsul of Africa, Caius Cornelius Rarus Sextius, although Quintus Pomponius Rufus had come to the proconsulship by the time of its completion in

110 A.D. The arch itself had two fluted Corinthian columns on each of its four faces and a similar column in each interior corner (Plates 25 and 26).

The great soldier-emperor Trajan was succeeded on the throne in 117 by one of the most interesting of ancient personalities, Hadrian. After having overcome the immediate problems of his succession and reviewed many of the provinces in the first of his great tours, Hadrian finally embarked for Africa in 128 A.D. This was only one phase of his over-all project of visiting as much as possible of his empire so as to see existing conditions at first hand. His wisdom suggested the propriety of personal contact with the Third Augustan Legion, on which depended the safety of Roman Africa. Traveling from Carthage to the Roman military camp, he there reviewed the forces and bestowed on them appropriate praise and encouragement. After about four months in Africa Hadrian returned to Rome during the summer, apparently having had no opportunity for visiting the cities of Tripolitania. Leptis did feel the effect of the imperial personality, however, through the predominating taste for classical forms which the emperor encouraged.

Heretofore, although in the first century A.D. classical forms did exert a certain influence over the structural design and architectural ornamentation in Leptis Magna, as well as throughout the other Roman cities of Tripolitania, the artistic and architectural flavor of this region was provincial and distinctively Tripolitanian. At Leptis the earlier imperial architectural structures were created of fine grey limestone, from the local quarries opened in the last years of the first century B.C.

When civic aspirations and prosperity called for the erection of a great public bath in the Leptis Magna of Hadrian's time, however, the architects and contractors, for the first time in the Roman history of Tripolitania, turned to marble as a structural and ornamental material. So strikingly attractive was the impression thus created that such a building as the Curia or local senate house, built, in the late first or early second century, to the east of the Forum Vetus atop a podium standing within a colonnaded court, represented the last of the old manner of construction.

As for the new baths, however, the site chosen lay in the southern quarter of the city above the banks of the Wadi Lebda (Plate 1), which had already been rechanneled so as to prevent floods within the city limits. In addition to this protection, other provisions were made to guarantee a permanent source of water. Although the dating of the various structures involved in this conception is difficult, the major elements must certainly have existed by the conclusion of the Hadrianic building activities in the second century, and all certainly must have been created by the end of the Severan period.

For the size of the population of Leptis Magna as it reached its greatest period of expansion during the first and second centuries after Christ, a mere blocking of the Wadi Lebda and the provision of catchment basins for the storage of rainwater was not enough. Traveling afield to the Wadi Caam, local engineers constructed a substantial concrete conduit which led water twelve miles overland to the Wadi Lebda, possibly joining it just below the great barrier dam constructed to divert water from the latter wadi into the channel circling to the west of the city. Here two reservoir buildings were created at some unknown date, and the conduit perhaps entered the northernmost one, which was divided into five vaulted cisterns.

The southernmost reservoir, comprising three vaulted cisterns and displaying external architectural ornamentation in the form of niches and doorways, may have been erected during the Severan period. In addition to these main sources of supply, at least the public baths in the town itself were provided with their own cisterns for storing rainwater, as well as water diverted from the public supply.

Scarce as water was in this sector of Africa, Leptis Magna had a fairly good rainfall and was favored by good wadis running from the watershed of the eastern Gebel range. Its citizens learned to draw upon all of these resources in order to maintain an adequate supply of water for indulging themselves in their taste for lovely public fountains and baths.

Safeguarded by these measures, the builders of the early second century A.D. commenced work on the great Hadrianic Baths which were finally dedicated and opened to the public in 127. With its main facade facing north, the Bath was comprised of a number of rooms arranged symmetrically along its north-south axis. The Roman bather entered from the north and immediately found himself in a large hall containing a swimming pool, or *natatio*, about ninety feet long and forty-eight feet wide, with a depth of about five and a half feet. The pool was surrounded on three sides by columns of pink breccia marble with Corinthian capitals. Three steps, surfaced with marble slabs, surrounded the pool and led down to the floor of the basin which was decorated with a mosaic imitation of gravel. The intake and outlet for the water was located beneath a stone base erected in the center of the pool's north side.

On either side of this main hall were situated reception halls or *atria*, and probably dressing rooms or *apodyteria*. From the main hall itself the bather passed through either one of two doors into a transverse corridor to the south. Crossing this he entered the large *frigidarium*, or cold room, sixty feet by about forty-nine feet in size, with a ceiling covered by cross-vaults in three sections carried by eight Corinthian columns having a height of about twenty feet. The entire hall was ornamented with marble walls and finely carved statues. In the east and west ends of the room were large openings which gave onto pools of cold water with black granite columns and various statues surrounding each pool (Plates 27 and 72).

Turning to the large arch in the centre of the *frigidarium's* southern wall, one passed through into the *tepidarium* or room for the warm bath. In small wings to the right and left two bathing pools were installed, possibly at a later date, while in the center of the chamber an archway opened onto a larger basin, square in shape, with two columns on both east and west sides and a wall on the southern side (Plate 28).

40

Passing behind the side columns and into the area behind the southern wall of the pool one entered a small vestibule from which one turned south again and walked on into the *calidarium* or hot room, the southernmost chamber in the bath structure. Measuring seventy-one and a half feet by about thirty-six feet, the *calidarium* was roofed with a barrel vault and had three large deep windows in the southern wall and one in each end wall. Later alterations led to the installation of water basins in each of the window areas, the largest basin forming a deep apse in the center of the south wall. Along the outside of this southern wall were ranged the furnaces for the *calidarium*. In the northwest and northeast corners of the *calidarium* itself doorways led into the *laconica* or sweat rooms, raised on false flooring to permit the circulation of hot air beneath. This air was heated by other furnaces again constructed against the south walls of these rooms.

Along the eastern and western sides of the entire bath structure there ranged a series of chambers which served perhaps as rest areas or meeting rooms. In the northeast corner of the building, near the Palaestra, provision was made for a colonnaded latrine, square in shape (Plate 29). As a form of large forecourt to the ensemble of rooms forming the bath establishment, a large Palaestra was erected with its long axis running in an east-west direction a bit to the east of the central axis of the baths themselves. This great Palaestra was surrounded with a portico and had a large apse or exedra at each end (Plates 30 and 31).

The great new public bath must have served considerably toward easing the discomfort of the hot north African daylight hours. Attracting weary citizens as well as those who merely wished to indulge themselves in a few hours of bathing and conversation, the baths became so well attended that repairs and further embellishments were inevitable. Important work of this nature was accomplished under the emperor Domitian (81–96 A.D.), while some furnishings, apparently minor in nature, were added in the time of Septimius Severus.

The employment of marble in this attractive and important Hadrianic building led the citizens of Leptis in the second century to consider altering other existing structures by replacing the older limestone elements with the newly-appreciated marble. The columns and pediment of the Temple of Rome and Augustus were rebuilt of marble, while almost the entire Temple of Liber Pater was redone in marble in the middle of the second century. The Theatre and the Chalcidicum also underwent phases of redecoration in the new material. On the southwest side of the Forum Vetus, at its northwest corner, a three-sided marble portico was constructed with a shrine in the court dedicated to the emperor Antoninus Pius (138–161 A.D.).

It was probably during the early years of the third century that the charming baths known as the Hunting Baths were established in the northwestern limits of the city above the foundations of some preexisting buildings. Built of rubble concrete, with ceilings in the form of domes and barrel-vaults, the baths are a remarkable expression of simple functional design fitting into the framework of the architectural use of concrete which developed in Rome during the first and early second centuries A.D. The Hunting Baths are completely unclassical in architectural execution and show a freedom of expression in design which removes them from the traditional pattern to be found in the Hadrianic Baths in the southeast quarter of Leptis Magna. Like these great baths, however, the Hunting Baths included the accepted Roman system of *apodyterium, frigidarium, tepidarium,* and *calidarium.*

Even with later additions the Hunting Baths did not match the Hadrianic Baths in size, but the fascinating wealth of mosaics and fresco decoration found in them, as well as details of the water storage and heating systems, lend these baths an importance which more than overcomes any disappointment in the small size of the structure. The Hunting Baths represent a medium-sized type of public bath ensemble which evidently found considerable vogue in the eastern Mediterranean and in Africa during these later years of the Roman empire. At least two other examples are to be found in Leptis Magna itself. The theme of the major decorations which give the name to the Hunting Baths suggests that this building may well have been owned at one time by a trade association of hunters.

During the years at the turn of the second and third centuries Leptis Magna was entering upon its last and greatest period of affluence. When the town's favorite son ascended the imperial throne in 193 A.D., as the emperor Septimius Severus, he carried with him a strong attachment to the African provinces and to Leptis Magna in particular. In Leptis his grandfather had been one of the two annual *suphetes* when Trajan raised the status of the town to that of a Roman colony. Thus this relative became one of the town's first two *duoviri* under the new constitution. Alhough Septimius' father, Publius Septimius Geta, was not of great importance locally, two of Septimius' uncles, Aper and Severus, were men of consular rank. Septimius himself left Leptis for Rome shortly after his eighteenth year but members of his family continued to reside in the town, and on one occasion when his sister visited him after his accession to the throne she embarrassed him in public by her inability to speak in Latin. The emperor himself always spoke Latin with a heavy African accent.

The early part of the reign of Septimius Severus was spent in suppressing several attempts made by other Roman generals to seize the throne. Interestingly enough Clodius Albinus, one of these aspirants, was also of African background, probably having been born at Hadrumetum. With these uprisings successfully quelled Septimius embarked upon his eastern campaigns against the Parthian kingdom. Immediately upon his victorious return to Rome in 202, which was commemorated by the erection of the arch dedicated to him in the Roman Forum, he made arrangements for a visit to his place of birth. At this time he granted to Leptis Magna the *ius Italicum,* which removed from the inhabitants the burden of tribute and land taxes. Out of respect and gratitude the city nevertheless provided for the continuance of its

42

annual payment of oil for the use of the citizens of Rome. In addition the magistrates, under direct imperial patronage, initiated a building program which was to make Leptis one of the most splendid cities of Roman Africa. The first evidence of this new program is found in the imposing four-sided arch, dedicated to Septimius Severus in 203 and erected over the crossroads of the two main streets of the city, the *Cardo* and the *Decumanus* (Plates 32, 33, and 34). With extremely elegant pilasters placed at each of the arch's four corners, the archways themselves were framed by Corinthian columns supporting broken pediments. On the very top of the arch were arranged four panels, one on each face, two of which depicted triumphal processions, one a sacrificial scene, and the last a domestic grouping of the imperial family. The details of the decoration suggest the craftsmanship of a designer trained in the architectural practices of the eastern Mediterranean. It is probable that the entire conception of the Severan embellishments of the city was due to the architects and craftsmen from the Greek or east Mediterranean area who came to Leptis for this purpose, importing for their work quantities of marble from Greek quarries.

Under the influence of this new school of thought the harbor of Leptis was enlarged and bounded by fine stone quays. A grand colonnaded street was laid out to connect the harbor with a splendid plaza just to the east of the Palaestra in front of the Hadrianic Baths. This plaza itself was dominated on the east side by a magnificently ornamented apse or Nymphaeum, highly decorated with marble veneer and several rows of columns superimposed one over the other. In order to provide additional area for the business and civic activities which had now outgrown the small Forum Vetus, a vast new Forum and Basilica compound was begun on the northwestern side of the colonnaded street. Completed in 216 A.D. during the reign of Caracalla, Septimius' son, this complex testifies to the great ingenuity of the Severan architects. Built on an irregularly-shaped plot of ground, the Forum still gave the appearance of conforming to the regular rectangular plan, with a Basicilica of good design and arrangements at its northeastern end. Differences of alignment were masked by *tabernae* or shops placed along the wall separating the Forum from the Basilica. An apse in the center of this wall contained a doorway which led, at a slight angle, into the Basilica. Three sides of the Forum were bordered by a colonnade supporting arches instead of the more standard horizontal architrave (Plates 37 and 38). Between the arches, on the flat surface above the columns, bas-reliefs of Nereid and Gorgon heads stood out in bold chiaroscuro (Plate 39).

On the fourth side of the Forum, to the southwest, stood a high podium bearing a square temple chamber, or *cella*, surrounded on both sides and the front by a red granite colonnade. This colonnade in the front was comprised of eight columns across the width with two inner rows of six columns each, thus leaving a comfortable space between the two center front columns and the door to the *cella*. The identification of this temple is probably to be made with the worship of the *genius* of the family of

43

Septimius Severus. Along the exterior of the Forum's southeast wall stood a row of shops, in the center of which an entranceway led into the Forum. Another such entrance in the northwestern wall corresponded to this.

The large Basilica at the northeast end of the Forum, measuring 290 by 120 feet, stood with its long axis running northwest to southeast. The interior was divided into a central nave and two side aisles by two rows of red granite Corinthian columns which supported upper galleries. Each end of the nave ended in a great apse decorated with columns and having a raised floor for the seats of officials (Plates 40 and 41). At each end of the side colonnades, both ground floor and gallery, a most ornate pilaster was affixed to the wall (Plate 42). Those on the main floor were carved with medallion-scrolls of acanthus interspersed with human, animal, and flower forms, while the four pilasters from the upper galleries bore ornamentations portraying the stories of Liber Pater and Hercules, the two patron deities of Leptis Magna. The entire area of the Basilica was roofed with wood and stairs were added behind the apses to provide access to the second floor galleries. Along the outer face of the Basilica's north wall a large passageway was created to link the colonnaded street with the section on the northwest side of the Basilica.

As for the harbor, which played such an important role in the commercial life of the town, the Severan architects conceived the idea of enlarging the promontory on the north side of the polygonal basin in order to construct or rebuild the Pharos or lighthouse. Corresponding to this, a watchtower was erected on the southern side of the harbor entrance, and near it a small Doric temple with a colonnaded porch. The eastern quays were formed in two levels, the upper one connected to the lower by small staircases and having on its face numerous stone mooring blocks. At least on this eastern side, a portico running along the upper level of the quay masked a variety of warehouses. On the southern side of the harbor there was evidently no true quay for the servicing of cargo ships, but rather a flight of shallow steps which led up to the level of a large temple, perhaps to be associated with Jupiter Dolichenus. The low western quay had short flights of steps leading right down to the water level of the port.

The entire building project of harbor, street, plaza, forum, and basilica was executed in brown limestone from the quarries at nearby Ras-el-Hammam, and the architects were not stinting in their creation of architectural ornamentation of marble from Euboea and the Greek islands as well as red and gray Egyptian granite. The completion of this vast program left Leptis Magna glistening in marbles, a brilliant Roman town reflecting its glory in the green-blue waters of the Mediterranean. The fickle rays of sunrise and sunset loaned colors of false fire to its walls. Buildings of great pride and humbler structures filling the blocks around gave protection, comfort, and shade to the busy citizens during the hot day, while marble and limestone warmed to the occasional light of torches and lanterns during the moonlit hours of the night. Greatness and beauty were here. Luxury bathing was to be had at little or no cost. Lusty or refined classical drama could be seen in the Theatre.

Noisy, thrilling contests with gladiators and wild African animals were continually scheduled in the Amphitheatre to the east of the city while here, too, the crowds could come to pour into one of the largest circuses in the Roman world. Measuring about 1462 feet by 325 feet, the Circus demonstrated the luxury taste of its builders by the row of five water basins running down the center of the course to form the *spina,* or wall, which divided the arena into two tracks.

But the magnificence of the new Leptis Magna had been obtained at the cost of stability. The town's treasuries had been strained to the limit to acquire this new appearance of grandeur. Such intense financial exhaustion now overtook Leptis as to carry it rapidly downhill to the point where it could never again attain the level of prosperity which had once belonged to it. The annual tribute of oil to Rome which the people of the city had willingly continued as a gift after the cancellation of this obligation by Septimius Severus soon became a great strain on the city's resources. Even with the increasing independence of the olive growers of the interior and the decrease in the city's population and wealth, this gift of oil came to assume once more the aspect of a required tribute. Not until the reign of Constantine was Leptis relieved of this burden. But this consideration could do nothing to save the city. The rigidity of societal structure and civic obligations established by the reforms of Diocletian had already begun to undermine the morale of the citizenry.

Some minor building activities were still undertaken during the first half of the fourth century, at which time new walls were built around the city which had already diminished in size. These walls, ruins of which may be seen on the west side of the city along with one of the city gates of the period, left much of the older city unprotected beyond its limits. The Hunting Baths were included in the section thus forsaken but they continued in use probably until the middle of the century. At this same time the Basilica Vetus on the Forum Vetus was severely damaged by a fire and extensively rebuilt under Constantine. The temple of unknown dedication on the southwest side of the Forum Vetus may well have been converted into a church before the middle of this century.

Life in Leptis Magna, however, was no longer secure, and its very existence was threatened when the Austuriani, a desert tribe to the southeast of Tripolitana, invaded the *limes* region and marched right down to the coast. There, somewhat overawed by the strong walls and the population of Leptis Magna, they pitched camp in the fields surrounding the city and for three days they ravaged the farms and nearby estates. Finally, leaving vast destruction behind them, they withdrew inland, taking with them as hostage one Silva, a magistrate of Leptis who had been visiting a country estate with his wife and children. Romanus, the *comes Africae,* led a unit of soldiers to the town after the Austuriani had departed, but after waiting forty days for the citizens to meet his impossible demands for supplies he finally withdrew his troops without accomplishing anything.

A direct appeal to the emperor Valentinian on the part of the governmental council of Tripolitana at first profited them nothing, and for a second time the desert tribes laid waste the city's surrounding lands. The lure was too great to be forgotten, and the Austuriani came back yet once more, this time invading the suburbs of Leptis and laying siege to its walls for eight days. Ultimately they packed their booty and marched southward again to their desert dwellings. With death and destruction on their doorsteps the citizens of Leptis found little consolation in the visit of several imperial inspectors to survey the situation. Evidently nothing constructive was done and the town merely retrenched its living area, giving up most of the dwellings outside the fourth-century city walls. Now the Hunting Baths in the western suburbs were completely abandoned.

With the coming of the Vandals, Tripolitana and its citizens were among the last to be taken into the barbarian kingdom, and the citizens of Leptis found little change and certainly no improvement in their economic condition. When the Byzantine army under Heraclius invaded Tripolitana probably in 468 or shortly thereafter, on its way to capture Carthage, the citizens of Leptis must have cheered on the soldiers as they marched along the coastal road. When this venture failed Leptis settled back once more into the growing obscurity of a little village. In 533 the citizens of the city once again heard the marching sound of a Byzantine army, but this time one destined to be victorious. Having united in the demonstration of revolt put forward by the whole region of Tripolitana, Leptis as well as the other coastal towns must have housed with pleasure the Byzantine forces sent to aid them. With the arrival of the great Belisarius and his forces off the coast south of Carthage, the Vandal kingdom was doomed and a certain flare of new life came to Leptis Magna.

Here as in other cities of Africa the Byzantine emperor Justinian encouraged the building of new fortifications and also churches to provide room for Christian services which had been greatly suppressed by the Vandals. The newly-reconstituted city was greatly diminished in size, as can be seen from the existing walls of this period which enclosed in their circuit the two forums, the harbor, and the intervening areas. These walls were built in part of stones removed from now-dilapidated buildings of the earlier imperial period, and it was at this time that the great Severan Basilica was converted into a Christian church. The spirit of ambition was gone from the citizens, however, and the encroaching sands proceeded to cover up the town's great past just as the vicissitudes of life had gradually overcome the morale of Roman life there. Liber Pater and Hercules withdrew into the shades of history, and when the new power of Islam first penetrated Tripolitana under the authority of 'Amr ibn-al-'As and then 'Abdullāh, in turn governors of Egypt for the Caliph Uthman (644–656

A.D.), Leptis Magna was nothing but a village. After the establishment of the Moham-
medan center at Al-Qayrawān, south of Carthage, in 670 by 'Uqbah ibn-Nāfi' and the
eventual conquest of Carthage and other Roman coastal towns in 698, Leptis was
deserted by its inhabitants and left to the engulfing sands.

3

THE TOWN OF SABRATHA

SITUATED ON THE Tripolitanian coast to the west of modern Tripoli, Sabratha was one of the ancient triad of cities, consisting of Sabratha, Oea (Tripoli), and Leptis Magna, which gave the name of Tripolitana to this territory. Like its two sister settlements Sabratha was in origin a mere Phoenician trading center, dating back perhaps to the seventh century B.C. The vestiges of this early outpost, situated between the harbor and the Forum, offer no evidence of solid permanent structures, but rather consist of the remains of Punic storage jars and Greek vases. This would indicate that the site was merely one where occasional traders stopped or might even have resided during the good sailing season. Eventually permanent structures of mud brick on foundations of stone were built during at least three periods of Punic control.

The citizens of this developing community were protected from native tribal attacks by a strong wall, the line of which was later used as the northern limit of the Forum. Due to the geographical conformation in this area of the coast, Sabratha was not in such close proximity to the rich olive-growing fields of the hinterland as was Leptis Magna. With only the suggestion of a protective harbor, guarded mainly by a reef just offshore, the citizens of Sabratha found little economic encouragement in the dry stretches of the Gefara plain which surrounded them. Their promise lay instead along the great trade route which ran inland from the town to the oasis of Ghadames. From there the way led into the Fezzan and the sources to the south from whence Sabratha derived the wild animals and exotic wares upon which her prosperity developed.

Sabratha, like Oea and Leptis Magna, was included in the commercial coastal area known, under Carthaginian control, as the Emporia. During the mid-second century B.C. Sabratha, along with all cities of the Emporia, passed into Numidian control, but little is known of the city's activities during this century or the next. The wars of Jugurtha and later of Julius Caesar certainly must have influenced the lives of the local citizenry, but it was the reorganization of Africa by Caesar that brought Sabratha into the new province of Africa Nova and the full aura of Roman culture. With prosperity and peace now encouraging the city toward expansion, new quarters were laid out beyond the limits already existing. To the south an imposing Forum developed over the complex of irregularly arranged buildings dating to the second century B.C., and to the east of the Forum new *insulae* or blocks of buildings were marked out during the first century A.D. For building stone the architects drew on the sandstone quarries to the southeast of the city. This material could not completely withstand the forces of erosion and so, for protection as well as aesthetic purposes, the architectural elements were covered with lime stucco which could be molded easily and painted (Plates 44 and 46).

At the northeast end of the Forum, the axis of which ran northeast to southwest, there was located a podium with a small temple on the top having moldings of painted stucco. This was probably constructed toward the end of the first century B.C. Directly opposite this temple and at the southwest end of the Forum stood the Capitolium, or the Temple of Jupiter, added to the Forum complex at some period shortly after the building of the former temple. This, perhaps the main temple of the city, stood on a great sandstone podium covered with stucco. The front of the podium was extended into the Forum to form a rostrum for public orators, who ascended to the upper level by means of a pair of stairways which flanked the podium. Behind the rostrum area a broad flight of steps led up to the main section on which the Temple of Jupiter was placed. The original stone pediment, walls, and columns surrounding the *cella* on the front and both sides were probably covered with stucco, while the *cella* or temple chamber proper appears to have been divided into three rooms by walls erected upon those within the podium below.

A Basilica, or hall for the public handling of legal matters, was erected on the southeast side of the Forum during Julio-Claudian or Flavian times (first century A.D.). This seems to have consisted of a rectangular hall surrounded on all sides with a colonnade. A tribunal, or large apse, opened off the center of the southeast side, and the main entrance leading out to the Forum stood opposite this.

It was probably during the reign of Augustus (died 14 A.D.) that the first Temple to Isis was built on the shore to the east of the city. It stood, like most of the other major temples at Sabratha, in a courtyard surrounded by porticos. Built on a podium, the *cella* was surrounded by a colonnade and was approached by a flight of steps in the front. Against the west wall of the courtyard stood five chapels, and at the east end of the enclosure access was had to the whole compound through a colonnaded entrance raised on steps. During the reign of Vespasian (69–79 A.D.), after the threatening turn of events between Oea and Leptis Magna in 69, this temple was reconstructed.

Although Leptis Magna was raised to the status of a colony by the emperor Trajan, it appears that the citizens of Sabratha retained their old Punic form of government, headed by two *suphetes,* until perhaps the reign of Antoninus Pius (138–161 A.D.), at which time Sabratha also was made a colony and the *suphetes* became *duoviri.* Oea did not receive this favor until about 164 A.D. The civic pride which prosperity and the new imperial recognition brought to the citizens of Sabratha, who now maintained shipping offices at Ostia on the Tiber, led them to emulate their sister city Leptis in refurbishing the public structures of their city.

Following the example of Leptis Magna, the architects of Sabratha imported quantities of Greek marble for their new works which appear to have been initiated

49

during the last half of the second century A.D. It was during this time or shortly afterward that the temple at the northeast end of the Forum was completely rebuilt on a larger scale (Plate 46). New marble Corinthian columns were also arranged to constitute porticos on the northwest and southeast sides of the Forum. The original pediment, columns, and steps of the Temple of Jupiter were rebuilt of marble, and various marble sculptures were installed in the temple at this time and later. In the southwest corner of the Forum a square building with cruciform interior also belongs to this period, as does the great temple precinct to the southeast of the Forum containing the so-called Antonine Temple (Plates 46 and 48). This latter compound was surrounded on three sides by a colonnade of columns carrying Corinthian capitals, and behind the southwest colonnade a grouping of rooms and a hall formed an impressive entranceway from the street. Against the northeast wall of the courtyard rose a high podium fronted by a flight of marble steps rising up to the temple proper. Four Corinthian columns supporting a marble entablature and pediment spanned the front of the temple, while a single column behind each of the end columns gave depth to the porch. The *cella* itself was ornamented on the exterior sides and front with fluted pilasters, the side pilasters being modeled in stucco while those in front were carved of marble. To the southwest of the Antonine Temple a second, unidentified temple compound was created in much the same fashion, but having no such elaborate entrance. Here the side colonnades differed somewhat in having a small apse at the southwestern end of each. Marble was used in paneling the floors and walls of these colonnades, although indications are that stucco may also have been employed at one time. The temple was set on a podium against the southwest wall of the courtyard, and here marble was used for the main steps and possibly the facade of the temple, although stucco appears on the sides of the podium.

Also approximately of the late second century may be the Temple of Serapis, located to the northwest of the Temple of Jupiter and just beyond the corner of the Forum. This temple complex followed the pattern of the others, having a colonnade on three sides, two in marble and one evidently in sandstone. Marble steps led to the top of the podium and the *cella* walls may have been ornamented with stucco pilasters on the exterior. When, toward the end of the second century A.D., the citizens of Sabratha extended their town planning into the area somewhat to the east of the older Forum and its surrounding quarters, they shifted the orientation of their structures to a truer north-south axis. Here, toward the end of the second century, a temple to Hercules was dedicated. Following the example of the other temples in Sabratha it was erected in a courtyard having Corinthian columns arranged in colonnades on the west, north, and east sides. At their southern ends the east and west colonnades each ended in an apse. While the floors and lower sections of the walls of these porticos were decorated with marble, the upper portions of the walls were ornamented with painted scenes. As for the temple itself, little remains to indicate its form as it stood against the south wall of the enclosure.

Southeast of the Temple of Hercules this late second-century quarter was embellished with a magnificent Roman theatre constructed basically of the local sandstone with protective covering and ornamentation of stucco. Designed in typical semicircular form with three superimposed rows of arches and pilasters to support the seats, the Theatre had an estimated capacity of five thousand people (Plates 53, 55, 58, 60, and 61). Beneath the seats two concentric corridors gave access, one to stairs which led to the upper seating area, the other to short radial passages going inward to the better seats nearer the orchestra (Plate 57). Important guests found entrance to their seats immediately around the orchestra by entering through passageways placed at either side of the auditorium and in front of the stage (Plate 69). A low stone screen separated these special seats from the rest of the audience. The front of the stage platform was ornamented with rectangular and semicircular niches containing ornamental bas-reliefs (Plates 70 and 71). At the back of the stage there were provided three entrances, each placed in a semicircular recess. A magnificent colonnade of columns with composite capitals stood in front of this rear wall, arranged in three stories and following the contour of the entire wall. A porch projected in front of each doorway (Plates 59, 68, and 69). The whole stage structure was protected by a ceiling sloping down toward the back and supported by great wooden beams.

A large room was situated at each side of the stage (Plates 57 and 69) and behind the stage itself a delightful garden was laid out with a portico of Corinthian columns on three sides. Such a portico or protected walk was an accepted part of classical theatre design, as we have already observed at Leptis Magna. Then, too, just as Leptis had an Amphitheatre, so did Sabratha. In the latter case it was located quite a distance to the east of the city and measured about 211 by 151 feet for the length and width of the arena. Two trenches were dug at right angles to one another in the center of the arena and a corridor ran around the circumference of the arena connecting various chambers where the animals were kept.

Although by the early years of the third century Sabratha had expressed its civic interests in a manner of which it could be proud, it had not led itself to that verge of financial disaster which Leptis Magna would reach under the Severan emperors. Sabratha gave birth to no emperor for whom it could feel obliged to attempt the impossible in architectural dedications. It was comfortably satisfied with having provided the lady Flavia Domitilla as wife to Vespasian (69–79 A.D.). Consequently the life of its citizen body ran on a fairly stable level throughout the third century and into the early years of the fourth century.

In the latter period the ever-present desire for more public buildings and structures could still be expressed in the construction of the portico which surrounded the East Forum Temple, at the northeast end of the Forum. At some time during this

51

century also the old Basilica on the southeast side of the Forum was changed to a basilica with central nave and two side aisles, an apse being constructed at each end just as in the Severan Basilica at Leptis Magna (Plate 46). Soon after this it was converted into a church.

Peace was destroyed, however, by the disastrous raids of the Austuriani in 363–365 A.D. who wrought great destruction in the very heart of Sabratha and compelled the initiation of a new building program. The native raiders had penetrated into the public squares of the city and had left in their wake many ruined and scarred public structures. Probably because of irreparable damage to the East Forum Temple at the northeast end of the Forum, a new white marble colonnade was erected across the front of the temple complex to separate it from the main area of the Forum. It may have been now that the old pagan Basilica on the southeast side of the Forum, where perhaps Apuleius of Madaura was tried for witchcraft, was converted into a Christian church, as already mentioned, and given a new front facing northeast. This completely cut off one-third of the old Basilica at this end. The width was also diminished by moving the northwest wall further in toward the center. This required a readjustment of the aisle colonnade on this side and the consequent reduction in the width of the nave. The columns on the aisles were replaced with paired columns. A baptistry for the new church was secured by altering the chamber behind the southwestern apse. Perhaps at this time also the adjacent building to the northwest, with cruciform interior, was changed somewhat to provide accommodations for meetings of the church officials. In this form its interior arrangement resembled a curia. Access to the adjoining church was provided by a doorway leading through the southeast wall.

Like the East Forum Temple at the northeast end of the Forum, the Temple of Jupiter was probably destroyed by the Austuriani and left in ruins by the citizens of the city who were now more interested in Christianity. The lack of inscriptions dating to the periods subsequent to the first half of the fourth century suggests this probability.

On the northwest side of the Forum a curia was erected in the fourth century to house the official meetings of the city magistrates. At least some work was done on the *atrium* of the Curia in the latter part of the century, as is clear from an inscription dedicated to Lucius Aemilius Quintus fil—for his efforts on behalf of the province, probably during the ravages of the middle of the century. The Curia itself is rectangular in form, with four broad steps rising from the center to the side walls on the northwest and southeast. These also run across the end of the room at the southwest. The city officials sat on seats placed upon these steps which, along with the walls, were ornamented with re-used marble from other structures. Pilasters decorated the side walls, while fully detached columns were ranged along the main southwest wall. Both pilasters and columns stood upon a projecting base which ran around the walls of the room. The *atrium* or entrance hall to the Curia was located at the northeast end and was entered from the street by a doorway in its southeastern wall. Opposite this entrance a large niche contained an apse formed in the northwest wall, and the entire *atrium* was provided with an interior colonnade of Corinthian columns as well as a rather coarse mosaic floor.

In that section of the city close to the edge of the water and north of the Theatre area, two additional Christian basilicas were erected during the later period. Built above the remains of earlier structures, the southernmost and largest of these two churches followed the standard basilica form with a baptistry added on the north end and a small courtyard to the east, surrounded by a colonnade and evidently utilizing an area formerly occupied by a series of bathing rooms. The more northern basilica was also typical in plan and was built over an earlier church, which in turn stood on the site of an unidentified rectangular structure.

Perhaps the best known Christian basilica in Sabratha is that built by order of the emperor Justinian and mentioned in the works of his courtier Procopius. This stood to the northwest of the Curia and the Forum. For its construction the builders drew upon ruins of pagan temples and early imperial monuments, some of which now stood outside the limits of the Byzantine city wall, built during the sixth century to protect the much-shrunken town of Sabratha. Of the usual basilica design, with nave and side aisles running along a northeast-southwest axis, the Justinianic Basilica had an external porch in front of the principal entrance at the southwest. In all probability there was an apse at the northeastern end of the interior as well as a pulpit, a canopied altar, and marble altar tables. Perhaps the most lovely item from this church, however, is the main floor of the nave done in mosaic to represent a vast number of birds of all descriptions moving casually amid the intertwining tendrils of grape vines. A magnificent peacock poses in a frame of vines at one end. The entire piece is a charming tour de force (Plates 96 and 97).

Aside from the public buildings mentioned above, Sabratha was dotted with a number of baths, among the largest of which was the Seaward Baths situated behind the East Forum Temple in the direction of the northern beach. Another bath establishment lay just east of the Temple of Hercules (Plate 44), while still another, the Oceanus Baths, was constructed to the northeast of the two Christian basilicas north of the Theatre (Plate 45). In building their homes the citizens of Sabratha faced a problem posed by the premium on good building lots. Forced by this situation to get the most usage out of a plot of ground, they frequently created second stories to their houses. In addition, the scarcity of water made it standard practice to install cisterns beneath the houses for the storage of rainwater (Plate 52).

With all of their greatness behind them, however, and in spite of the encouragement offered by the emperor Justinian in his attempt to revive Roman life in Africa, the citizens of Sabratha lost their lust for living and ability to continue building their city and culture after continuous military upheavals in the country. When the Byzantine walls were erected in the sixth century the city had already been reduced to the area of the Forum and its surrounding city blocks. The sand was beginning to overcome the town and finally, with the advent of the Moslems, it was left all but deserted. Like Leptis Magna it could not attain that continuity of existence which fell to the lot of the sole survivor Oea, the modern Tripoli.

BIBLIOGRAPHY

ALBERTINI, EUGENE (revised by Louis Leschi). *L'Afrique Romaine*. Oxford, 1940.

BARTOCCINI, RENATO. *Guida di Lepcis*. Rome, 1927(?).

———. *Guida di Sabratha*. Rome, 1927.

———. "Il Foro Imperiale di Lepcis (Leptis Magna)," in *Africa Italiana*, Vol. I, no. 1. Bergamo, 1927.

———. "Il Foro Imperiale di Lepcis (Leptis Magna)," in *Africa Italiana*, Vol. II, no. 1. Bergamo, 1928.

CAMPS-FABRER, HENRIETTE. *L'Olivier et l'Huile dans l'Afrique Romaine*. Algiers, 1953.

Cambridge Ancient History, Vols. IX and X.

CAPUTO, G., and DELLA VIDA, G. LEVI. "Il Teatro Augusteo di Leptis Magna Secondo Lo Ultime Scoperte e un' Iscrizione Bilingue in Latino e Neo-Punico," in *Africa Italiana*, Vol. VI, nos. 3 and 4. Bergamo, 1935.

CARY, M. *The Geographic Background of Greek and Roman History*. Oxford, 1949.

CASSERLY, GORDON. *Tripolitania*. London, 1943.

CHARLES-PICARD, GILBERT. *Les Religions de l'Afrique Antique*. Paris, 1954.

COURTOIS, CHRISTIAN. *Les Vandales et l'Afrique*. Paris, 1955.

DELLA VIDA, G. LEVI. "Due Iscrizioni Imperiali Neopuniche di Leptis Magna," in *Africa Italiana*, Vol. VI, nos. 1 and 2. Bergamo, 1935.

GOODCHILD, R. G., and PERKINS, J. B. WARD. "The Limes Tripolitanus in the Light of Recent Discoveries," *Journal of Roman Studies*, Vol. XXXIX (1949), pp. 81-95.

———. "The Limes Tripolitanus, II," *Journal of Roman Studies*, Vol. XL (1950), pp. 30-38.

———. "Roman Sites on the Tarhuna Plateau of Tripolitania," *Papers of the British School at Rome*, Vol. XIX (new series, Vol. VI) (1951), pp. 43-77.

———. "Roman Tripolitania: Reconnaissance in the Desert Frontier Zone," *The Geographical Journal*, Vol. CXV, nos. 4-6 (June, 1950), pp. 161-178.

———. "Two Monumental Inscriptions of Lepcis Magna," *Papers of the British School at Rome*, Vol. XVIII (new series, Vol. V) (1950), pp. 72-82.

GUIDI, GIACOMO. "Criteri e Metodi Seguiti per il Restauro del Teatro Romano di Sabratha," in *Africa Italiana*, Vol. VI, nos. 1 and 2. Bergamo, 1935.

———. "La Data di Costruzione della Basilica di Leptis Magna," in *Africa Italiana*, Vol. II, no. 4. Bergamo, 1929.

———. "Orfeo, Liber Pater e Oceano in Mosaici della Tripolitania," in *Africa Italiana*, Vol. VI, nos. 3 and 4. Bergamo, 1935.

55

———. "Il Teatro Romano di Sabratha," in *Africa Italiana,* Vol. III, nos. 1 and 2. 1930.

PARKER, H. M. D. *The Roman Legions.* Oxford, 1928.

PERKINS, JOHN B. WARD. "The Arch of Septimius Severus at Lepcis Magna," *Archaeology,* Vol. 4, no. 1 (1951), pp. 226-231.

———. "The Hunting Baths at Lepcis Magna," *Archaeologia,* Vol. XCIII (1949), pp. 165-195 (written with the cooperation of J. M. C. Toynbee).

———. "Severan Art and Architecture at Lepcis Magna," *Journal of Roman Studies,* Vol. XXXVIII (1948), pp. 59-80.

———. "Tripolitania and the Marble Trade," *Journal of Roman Studies,* Vol. XLI (1951), Parts I and II, pp. 89-104.

ROMANELLI, PIETRO. "Leptis Magna," in *Africa Italiana,* Vol. I. Rome, 1925.

———. *Il Limes Romano In Africa.* Istituto di Studi Romani, 1939.

———. "La Prima Linea di Difesa di Leptis Magna," *Archeologia Classica,* Vol. IV (1952), pp. 100-102.

ROSTOVTZEFF, M. *The Social and Economic History of the Roman Empire.* Oxford, 1926.

WARMINGTON, B. H. *The North African Provinces From Diocletian to the Vandal Conquest.* Cambridge, 1954.

PLATES

Plate 1   LEPTIS MAGNA

Aerial view looking east over the town. In middle distance is the Wadi Lebda with the harbor at its mouth to the left. The Forum Vetus is at left center, with the Theatre, the Market, and the Chalcidicum grouped in the lower left. In the center can be seen the Forum of Severan times with the Basilica and, to the right, the Nymphaeum. In the center right are the Hadrianic Baths and the Palaestra, with the Arch of Septimius Severus in the lower right.

Plate 2

LEPTIS MAGNA

Aerial view looking northeast over the Theatre, with the Chalcidicum to its right. Beyond the Chalcidicum is the Market and in the upper right are the Severan Forum and Basilica.

Plate 3

LEPTIS MAGNA

View of arches forming the southeastern entrance to the Market. Through the arch can be seen columns of the interior portico, and to the left are the columns surrounding one of the *tholoi* or circular buildings in which sales counters were arranged.

Plate 4   LEPTIS MAGNA

View of the arches forming the entrance at the southeastern end of the Market. In the background is the southwest perimetal wall.

Plate 5   LEPTIS MAGNA

Architrave block over the entrance to the court or chamber at the southeast end of the stage of the Theatre. The inscription dates the erection of the Theatre to the thirteenth consulship of Augustus and names the donor as Annobal, the embellisher of his city or state.

Plate 6   LEPTIS MAGNA

    View along the street leading to the southeast entrance of the Theatre. To the left are the ruins of the Chalcidicum, while in the distance is the architrave block bearing the inscription of Annobal, builder of the Theatre. To the left, beyond the Chalcidicum, can be seen the upper part of the Theatre with portions of the colonnade which ran along the top of the semicircular wall.

Plate 7

LEPTIS MAGNA

The Theatre as seen from the southwest, showing the extremely simple ornamentation of the outer wall supporting the seats.

Plate 8   LEPTIS MAGNA

Interior of the Theatre with the seats ranging upward from the semicircular orchestra, around which can be seen the low steps on which seats were placed for important members of the audience. To the left are ruins of the walls which supported the wooden stage and behind them the colonnade of the *scaenae frons* or ornamental back wall.

Plate 9

LEPTIS MAGNA

View showing the seats of the Theatre with the exits leading down to corridors under the seats. At the left are sections of the colonnade and the statue of Ceres, which was situated in a small shrine at this point.

Plate 10   LEPTIS MAGNA

The location in the Theatre where the Temple or Shrine to Ceres was placed. A statue of this goddess is shown resting on a base projecting into the seating area of the auditorium.

Plate 11   Leptis Magna

The northwestern end of the auditorium of the Theatre. Capitals and bases of columns now missing are placed here on the upper row of seats. In the distance is the Mediterranean.

Plate 12   LEPTIS MAGNA

The upper stories of the Theatre's outer wall, with some columns of the upper colonnade replaced in position.

Plate 13   LEPTIS MAGNA

View looking northwest across end wall of the Chalcidicum and its exterior colonnade toward the outer wall of the Theatre.

The southeastern section of the Theatre's outer wall, with a colonnade to the right along the northwest wall of the Chalcidicum enclosure.

Plate 15   LEPTIS MAGNA

The southeastern section of the Theatre's outer wall as seen from the street to the southwest of the Chalcidicum. In the foreground is the west corner of the Chalcidicum, with a section of the colonnade which was later enclosed to form a cistern.

Plate 16   LEPTIS MAGNA

Aerial view showing the Theatre at left center with the colonnaded portico behind the stage building. At bottom center is the Chalcidicum enclosure, with its colonnaded front opening onto the Cardo or main north-south street which crosses the lower right corner of the picture. At right center is the Market, with its two eight-sided structures for the display of foods on sale.

Plate 17

LEPTIS MAGNA

The stage of the Theatre as seen looking across to the southeast entrance. The three low walls which supported the wooden stage floor can be seen here in front of the fine marble colonnade which decorated the rear wall. The recesses in the colonnade indicate entrances to the stage.

Plate 18   LEPTIS MAGNA

Ruins of the stage in the Theatre looking toward the northwestern exit. The columns form part of the portico which ornamented the rear wall, while at the right can be seen one of the Theatre's decorative statues.

View of the stage in the Theatre as seen from the floor of the orchestra. Immediately in front are the niches which ornamented the front wall supporting the wooden stage. A marble statue stands in one of these, while to the left can be seen an exit with the architrave block carrying an inscription of Annobal Rufus, the builder of the Theatre.

Plate 20   LEPTIS MAGNA

The stage of the Theatre as viewed from the upper row of seats at the western side of the auditorium. The recesses formed by the stage colonnade or portico indicate apses in the back wall where doorways were located for entrance upon the stage. In the distance are ruins of the Forum Vetus and the northern promontory of the harbor, with the Mediterranean in the background.

Plate 21

LEPTIS MAGNA

View of the Theatre stage from one of the auditorium entrances in the western section. The niches along the front supporting wall of the stage floor can be seen with a marble statue occupying one of these.

Plate 22   LEPTIS MAGNA

The columned portico of the Chalcidicum facing on the Cardo. At the right is the platform projecting in front of the small temple situated in the center of the row of shops behind the colonnade.

Plate 23   LEPTIS MAGNA

  View of the columns on the platform located in front of the small temple in the main south-east entrance colonnade of the Chalcidicum. Behind the columns lie the fragments of the archi-trave which mentions Chalcidicum as the name of the structure. In the distance is the southeast wall of the Theatre.

Plate 24   LEPTIS MAGNA

The main southeast colonnade of the Chalcidicum entrance, with ruins of shop walls immediately behind. Beyond is the interior of the Chalcidicum compound, with the southeast wall of the Theatre in the distance.

Plate 25

LEPTIS MAGNA

The Arch of Trajan as seen from the southwest, spanning the Cardo. Beyond is the less elaborate Arch of Tiberius and behind it, to the left, the arched entrance to the Market.

83

Plate 26   LEPTIS MAGNA

View looking northeast along the Cardo to the Arch of Trajan and, beyond, the Arch of Tiberius.

The western pool in the *frigidarium* of the Hadrianic Baths showing, at the right, one of the niches which contained ornamental marble sculptures.

Plate 28   LEPTIS MAGNA

Detail of the stone archway over the entrance to the pool in the center of the *tepidarium* of the Hadrianic Baths. Behind it is the arched doorway leading from the *frigidarium*.

86

Plate 29

LEPTIS MAGNA

The latrine in the northeast corner of the Hadrianic Baths.

Plate 30   LEPTIS MAGNA

View of the Palaestra in front of the Hadrianic Baths looking toward the Nymphaeum of the Severan period. To the right is the northern facade of the Hadrianic Baths.

Eastern end of the Palaestra showing the semicircular form of the colonnade. In the background is the Severan Nymphaeum with an archway opening onto the great colonnaded street which led down to the harbor. To the left are the ruins of the Severan Forum.

Plate 32

LEPTIS MAGNA

View looking northwest along the street leading to the four-way Arch of Septimius Severus, which can be seen with several columns restored to their proper positions. In the far distance is the West Gate Arch leading through the fourth-century wall of the city.

Plate 33

LEPTIS MAGNA

The southwestern side of the four-way Arch of Septimius Severus.

Plate 34 LEPTIS MAGNA

The southwestern side of the Arch of Septimius Severus, showing the Arch of Trajan across the Cardo in the distance.

Plate 35

LEPTIS MAGNA

Inscription to Augusta Salutaris atop the northwest wall of the Cardo, just northeast of the four-way Arch of Septimius Severus which it once adorned.

Plate 36   LEPTIS MAGNA

Inscription dedicated to Augusta Salutaris by Caius Vibius Marsus, shown here on the Cardo, northeast of the four-way Arch of Septimius Severus to which it belongs.

Plate 37   Leptis Magna

Interior of the Severan Forum looking toward the Basilica at the northeast end. Along the lower edge of the Basilica wall can be seen the doorways of the shops, or *tabernae,* which lined this side of the Forum. At the extreme left is the apse containing the entrance leading into the Basilica, while on the right are the arches and column capitals belonging to the colonnade which surrounded the Forum.

Plate 38 LEPTIS MAGNA

The reconstituted arches of the southeastern section of the colonnade surrounding the Severan Forum. Between the arches are inserted the heads of Nereids and Gorgons, while on the ground in front have been arranged portions of the decorative scrollwork and moldings which ran along the arcade above the carved heads.

Plate 39

LEPTIS MAGNA

One of the Gorgon heads on the southeastern arcade of the Severan Forum.

Plate 40

LEPTIS MAGNA

View looking toward the southeastern apse of the Severan Basilica, showing the ground-floor colonnades and the elaborate terminal pilasters. At the right is the doorway leading into the Forum.

Plate 41   LEPTIS MAGNA

Interior of the Severan Basilica, showing the northwestern apse at the left and portions of both ground-floor colonnades.

Plate 42 LEPTIS MAGNA

A portion of the northeastern colonnade of the Severan Basilica near the apse at the north-western end, showing the architrave carrying the dedicatory inscription to the emperor Septimius Severus.

Plate 43 SABRATHA

View looking eastward along the coast toward Sabratha. In the center rises the stage building of the Theatre.

Plate 44

SABRATHA

Aerial view of the town showing the Theatre at right center, with the Temple of Isis on the coast to the right. On the left is the Forum, with the standing columns of the East Forum Temple, and adjacent to this precinct the courtyard of the Antonine Temple with the temple podium. Just off shore to the left is the reef which gave some protection to the beach where vessels could be drawn up.

Plate 45   SABRATHA

Aerial view looking westward over the town. In the foreground along the coast is the Temple of Isis, and directly above it the Oceanus Baths. To the left center is the Theatre and above it, on the shore, the site of the Forum and the old Phoenician town settlement.

Plate 46   SABRATHA

The Forum looking toward the southwest end where the Temple of Jove or Jupiter is located, with the Temple of Serapis to the right of it. On the right side of the Forum square is the Curia and beyond it, toward the sea, the Justinianic Basilica. In the right foreground stand the ruins of the East Forum Temple within its courtyard, and to the left of it is the enclosure of the Antonine Temple. Above this temple is the Christian church formed from the old Basilica, one apse of which can be seen.

Plate 47   SABRATHA

At the left center are the columns standing on the southeast wall of the podium of the East Forum Temple, while in the left foreground are columns from the Forum's southeast portico.

Plate 48

To the left are columns on the southeast podium wall of the East Forum Temple as seen from the inside of the podium. In the center distance stands the podium of the Antonine Temple.

Plate 49   SABRATHA

The Forum as seen looking northwest over the adjacent ruins. At right center is the East Forum Temple.

Plate 50

View looking northwest toward the Forum. Just in front of the columns of the East Forum Temple, in the center, are lower sections of the Antonine Temple. The pilasters in stone and stucco can be seen decorating the temple's southeast wall.

Plate 51   SABRATHA

The opening or gate in the Byzantine wall, showing the Forum ruins and the East Forum Temple in the distance.

Plate 52

SABRATHA

The sunken court and surrounding colonnade of a private house to the southwest of the Theatre.

Plate 53   SABRATHA

View looking northeast toward the Theatre, with the colonnaded court of a private house at the left.

Plate 54   SABRATHA

The southwestern wall of the Theatre auditorium as seen through the courtyard colonnade of a private house, also shown in Plates 52 and 53.

Plate 55

SABRATHA

View looking down into the supporting walls and corridors beneath the seats of the Theatre.

Plate 56   SABRATHA

Interior of the Theatre auditorium with the orchestra and special seating area to the left. Also visible are the exits leading to the corridors beneath the seats.

114

Plate 57   SABRATHA

Aerial view of the Theatre from the southeast, with the Forum in the distance.

Plate 58   SABRATHA

The Theatre as viewed from the southwest, with the courtyard colonnade of a private house to the right.

Plate 59

View looking northeast from the seating area of the Theatre toward the back wall of the stage.

Plate 60   SABRATHA

The exterior wall of the Theatre auditorium as seen from the west.

Plate 61   SABRATHA

The southwestern section of the auditorium wall of the Theatre, showing the ground-floor arches giving access to the corridors and stairs beneath the seats.

Plate 62   Sabratha

View into the peripheral corridor beneath the seats on the western side of the Theatre.

Plate 63

The west end of the *scaenae frons*, or decorative back wall of the stage in the Theatre, as seen from beneath the seats of the auditorium.

Plate 64   SABRATHA

The Theatre as seen from the south looking over the ruins of the auditorium toward the stage.

Plate 65   SABRATHA

The west face of the Theatre auditorium, showing the arrangement of arches for supporting the seats and also for providing access to the interior corridors.

Plate 66   SABRATHA

View looking north through the ruins of the seats in the auditorium toward the *scaenae frons* or stage of the Theatre.

Plate 67   SABRATHA

Looking northwest toward the stage of the Theatre, with the entrance archways to the auditorium seats in the middle distance.

Plate 68   SABRATHA

The *scaenae frons,* the stage, and the orchestra of the Theatre. The decorative frieze on the front wall supporting the wooden stage can be clearly seen. In front of the back wall on the stage is the beautiful three-tiered colonnade masking the wall itself. This latter has three recesses which contain entrances to the stage, ornamented in front with small columned porches.

Plate 69   SABRATHA

The stage of the Theatre viewed from its western end. To the left is the *scaenae frons* and at the far end of the stage the side entrance. To the right of the latter, on the level of the orchestra, is the entrance for visitors sitting in the special section around the orchestra.

Plate 70   SABRATHA

One of the decorated niches in the supporting wall along the front of the stage in the Theatre.

Plate 71

Decorative frieze in one of the niches ranged along the front supporting wall of the wooden stage in the Theatre. The subject is the Judgment of Paris.

Plate 72

Antinous-type statue from the *frigidarium* of the Hadrianic Baths at Leptis Magna.

130

Plate 73

Statue of Artemis of Ephesus found near the Circus at Leptis Magna.

Plate 74

Imperial statue found at Leptis Magna showing close view of the detail on the cuirass.

Plate 75

Marble statue of a goddess from Leptis Magna.

Plate 76

Marble portrait heads for insertion in statues. Both are Julio-Claudian figures found at Leptis Magna. To the left is Drusus, while the one on the right may be Germanicus. The heads come from the Temple of Rome and Augustus in the Forum Vetus.

Plate 77

Marble statue of a god or hero carrying a spear in the left hand.

Plate 78

Marble statues and a Punic inscription from a *tholos* in the Market at Leptis Magna.

Plate 79

Marble statue of Athena wearing her helmet and aegis, with a spear in her left hand and an owl resting on her right forearm. A shield stands against her left leg. The statue is from Leptis Magna.

Plate 80

Marble statue from Leptis Magna showing a god holding an infant on his right knee, while a turtle attempts to crawl out from under his right foot.

Plate 81

Statue of Aphrodite, from Leptis Magna, with a dolphin on her right side carrying an eros.

Plate 82

Marble portrait statue of a magistrate from Leptis Magna.

Plate 83

Reconstruction of the Exedra of Septimius Severus in the Forum Vetus at Leptis Magna, with statues and a mosaic from the same city.

141

Plate 84

Mosaic, fragments of statues, and portrait heads from Leptis Magna.

Plate 85

Mosaic from Leptis Magna in the region just to the north of the Palaestra, showing scenes of farm life and fishing activities with a picture at the top of Orpheus surrounded by animals.

Plate 86

Portrait head of Augustus from the Temple of Rome and Augustus at Leptis Magna.

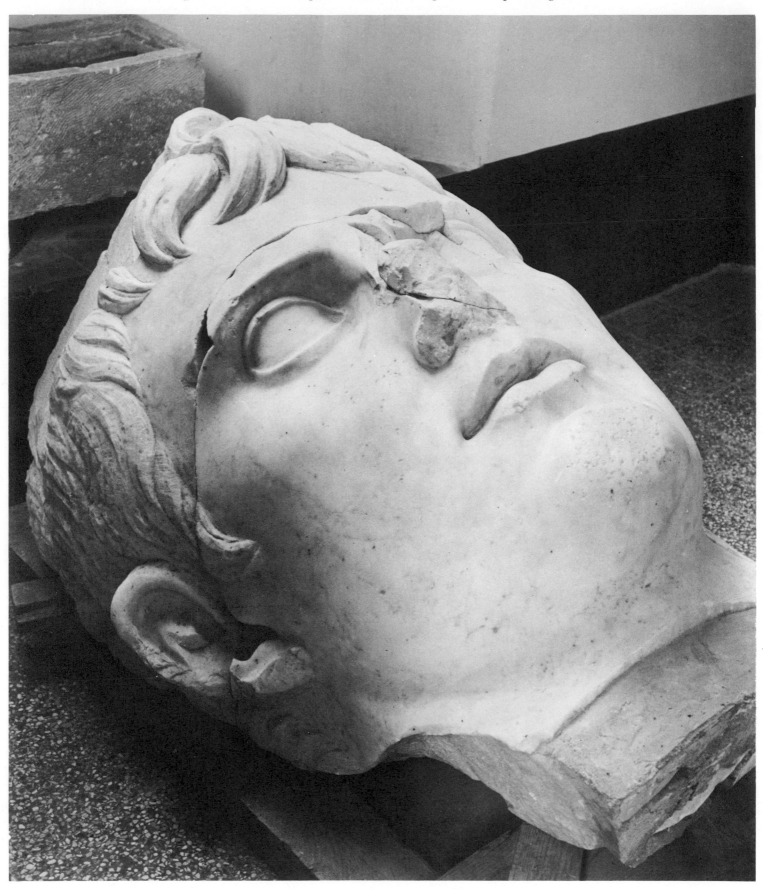

Plate 87

Portrait head of Tiberius from the Temple of Rome and Augustus at Leptis Magna.

Plate 88

Julio-Claudian portrait head.

146

Plate 89

A group of three marble statues from Leptis Magna, with a copy of Polycleitus' "Diadumenus" in the center. At the right is a copy of the "Faun" by Praxiteles and to the left a statue of the Omphalos-Apollo type. Above is an allegorical mosaic of the Nile from the Nile villa.

Plate 90

Mosaic.

Plate 91

Mosaic from the house of Liber Pater at Sabratha, showing animal heads and the triumph of Dionysus.

149

Plate 92

Mosaic decoration from the Oceanus Baths at Sabratha.

Plate 93

Mosaics from Sabratha. At the upper left are two floor decorations in mosaic from the bathing establishment just east of the Temple of Hercules. These show items used for the bath, such as strigils for scraping the skin clean. In addition there are the two statements that bathing keeps one healthy and also the wish that one should have a good bath.

Plate 94

Bust of the goddess Concordia found in the Temple of Jupiter at Sabratha.

Plate 95

Statue of the goddess Coelestis found in the Temple of Jupiter at Sabratha.

153

Plate 96

Mosaics and column bases from the Justinianic Basilica at Sabratha.

154

Mosaic from the nave of the Justinianic Basilica at Sabratha.

INDEX

Abaritana, the, 30
'Abdullāh, 46
Adherbal, 19
Aemilius, Iddibal Caphada, 36
Africa, diocese of North, 26
Africa Nova, 20, 48
Africa Proconsularis, 19, 20, 22, 24, 25, 28, 30, 31
Africa Vetus, 20
Agriculture, 17, 19, 23, 25, 26, 33, 34, 36, 37
Alans, 30
Alaric, 29
Albinus, Clodius, 42
Al-Qayrawan, 32, 47
Ammaedara, 22, 25
Ammicar, 34
Ampsaga River, 20
'Amr ibn-al-'Ās, 46
Annona, 19, 23, 26, 27
Antoninus Pius, 41, 49
Antony, Mark, 20
Anullinus, 28
Aper, Publius Septimius, 42
Apuleius of Madaura, 52
Arcadius, 27
Arians, 31
Arles, Council of, 29
Assyrians, 17
Attalus, 29
Augustus, 20, 34, 35, 37, 41, 49
Austuriani, the, 27, 45, 46, 52

Bacchus, 34
Balearic Islands, 31
Basiliscus, 30
Bathanarius, 27, 29

Belisarius, 31, 46
Bocchus of Mauretania, 19
Boniface, 29, 30
Britain, 28
Bu-Ngem, 24, 25
Byzacena, 25, 30-32

Caecilian, 28, 29
Caesar, Julius, 19, 20, 34, 48
Caligula (*see* Gaius)
Camel, use of, 33
Caracalla, 24, 43
Carthage, 17, 19, 20, 23, 26, 28, 30-33, 39, 46-48
Carthage, Bishop of, 28, 29
Carthage, Conference of, 29
Cavalry, African, 27
Chad, Lake, 33
Church, the Christian, 28, 29, 31, 46, 52, 53
Churches, 45, 46, 52, 53
Circumcelliones, 29
Cirta, 19, 20, 30
Claudius, 23, 34
Cleopatra VII of Egypt, 20
Cleopatra Selene, 20
Coloni, 23, 24
Comes Africae, 27, 29, 45
Commerce, 17, 20, 22, 23, 26, 33, 37, 48, 49
Constantine, 27-29, 45
Constantinople, 27, 31
Constantius, 28
Consulares, 31
Corsica, 31
Curia (*see Curiales*, Leptis Magna *and* Sabratha), 26, 27

156

Curiales, 28
Cyrenaica, 20, 25, 33

Diocletian, 25-28, 31, 45
Dolabella, Publius, 22
Domain, African imperial, 24
Domitian, 38, 41
Domitilla, Flavia, 51
Donatists, 29
Donatus, 29
Duoviri, 38, 42, 49
Dux, 26, 27, 32

Emporia, 17, 19, 22, 48
Engineers, 20, 37, 39
Eudoxia (empress), 30
Eudoxia (daughter of empress), 30
Exarchate, 32

Festus, Valerius, 38
Fezzan, the, 33, 48
Firmus, 27, 29
Foederati, 30
Fortifications (*see* Military stations), 24, 25,
    27, 32, 39, 46
Fosse, 25

Gabes, Gulf of, 33
Gaetulia, 30
Gaiseric, 30
Gaius (Caligula), 22, 23, 26
Galba, 23
Galerius, 28
Garamantes, 22, 23, 33, 38
Gasr Duib, 25
Gauda of Numidia, 19
Gaul, 28, 29
Gebel escarpment, 24, 33, 40
Gebel road, 25
Gefara, plain of the, 33, 48
Gelimer, 31
Gemellae, 25
Germanus, 31

Geta, Publius Septimius, 42
Ghadames, 24, 48
Gheria el-Garbia, 24, 25
Gibraltar, 32
Gildo, 27, 29
Goths, 29
Governor of Africa, proconsular, 19, 20, 22,
    23, 26, 28, 29, 36, 38
Grain, 23, 25-27, 38
Grain dole, 19, 26
Grapes, 19

Hadrian, 23, 25, 39
Hadrumetum, 17, 42
Heraclian, 29
Heraclius, 30, 46
Hercules, 34, 44, 46
Hiempsal, 19
Hippo, 30
Honorius, 27, 29
Horrea, 26

Iddibale, 34
Italy (*see* Ostia *and* Rome), 26, 29, 30

Juba I, 20
Juba II, 20
Jugurtha, 19, 48
Julian, 29
Justinian, 31, 32, 46, 53

Lambaesis, 22, 23, 25
Lamia, Lucius Aelius, 36
Land investors, 23
Legate: of proconsul of Africa, 26; of Third
    Augustan Legion, 20, 22, 26
Legions (*see Limitanei*): Diocletian's re-
    forms, 26, 27; First Macrianan, 23;
    Ninth Hispanic, 22; replaced by native
    farmers in Tripolitania, 25; Third Au-
    gustan, 20, 22-26, 38, 39
Leo, 30

Leptis Magna, 17, 19, 20, 22-25, 27, 28, 33-47, 48, 49, 51, 54
    Amphitheatre, 45
    Arch: of Flavian period, 38; of Septimius Severus, 43; of Tiberius, 35, 37; of Trajan, 38, 39
    Architects of, 37, 39, 40, 43, 44
    Bacchus, 34
    Basilica: Severan, 43, 44, 46, 52; Vetus, 34, 35, 45
    Baths: Hadrianic, 39, 40, 41, 42; Hunting, 41, 42, 45, 46
    Cardo, 35, 36, 38, 43
    Chalcidicum, 36, 38, 41
    Churches, 45, 46
    Circus, 45
    City walls, 27, 37, 38, 45, 46
    Civitas libera, 37
    Coinage, 37
    Colonia Ulpia Traiana Leptis, 38
    Curia, 39
    Decumanus, 43
    Forum: Severan, 43, 44, 46; Vetus, 34-39, 41, 43, 45, 46
    Harbor, 43, 44, 46
    Hercules, 34, 44, 46
    Ius Italicum, 42
    Magistrates, 19, 37, 38, 42, 43, 45
    Market, 35
    Monticelli, 37, 38
    Municipium, 37
    Nymphaeum, 43
    Palaestra, 41
    Pharos, 44
    Portico dedicated to Antoninus Pius, 41
    Quarries, 39, 43, 44
    Rome and Augustus, cult of, 34, 41
    Temple: of Ceres, 36; of Jupiter Dolichenus, 44; of Liber Pater, 34, 41; of Magna Mater, 38; to genius of family of Septimius Severus, 43, 44
    Theatre, 35, 36, 41, 45
    Wadi: Caam, 39; Lebda, 33, 34, 37, 39, 40; er-Rsaf, 37
    Water system, 37, 39, 40
Liber Pater, 34, 41, 44, 46
Limes: Tripolitanus, 25, 45; Tentheitanus, 25; in Tunisia, 25
Limitanei, 25, 27, 32
Liturgies, 26

Maccomades (Sirte), 25
Macer, Clodius, 23
Magister equitum, 27
Magister militum, 31, 32
Majorinus, 29
Masinissa of Numidia, 17, 19
Mauretania, 19, 20, 22, 23, 32; Caesariensis, 27, 30-32; Sitifensis, 25, 27, 29-32; Tingitana, 31
Mauri, 22
Maurice, 32
Maxentius, 28
Maximian, 27, 28
Merchants, 20
Mesphe (Medina Doga), 24, 37
Military road: in Tripolitania, 24, 25, 36, 37; in Tunisia, 24
Military stations (*see* Fortifications), in Tripolitania, 24, 25
Mizda, 25
Moslems, 32, 46, 47, 54
Musulamii, 22

Native tribes of Africa (*see* Abaritana, Austuriani, Gaetulia, Garamantes *and* Musulamii), 17, 20, 22-24, 27, 30-33, 37, 38, 45, 46, 48, 52
Navicularii, 26
Nero, 23, 24, 37
Niger river, 33
Numidia, 17, 19, 20, 22, 25, 26, 28-32, 48

Oea (Tripoli), 17, 19, 20, 22, 24, 25, 27, 30, 33, 37, 38, 48, 49, 54

Olives, 19, 33, 48
Olive oil, 19, 23, 26, 33, 34, 43, 45
Ostia, 49

Pannonia, 22
Persecutions, Christian, 28
Phoenician elements, 17, 19, 22, 33, 34, 37, 48, 49
Piso, Cnaeus Calpurnius, 34
Placidia (daughter of empress Eudoxia), 30
Placidia, Galla, 29
Police force at Carthage, 22
Pompey, Cnaeus, 20
Praefectus annonae Africae, 26
Praepositi horreorum, 26
Praepositus, 25
Praeses, 26, 31, 32
Praetorian praefect, 26, 31
Procopius, 53
Ptolemy of Mauretania, 23
Punic wars, 17, 19

Quintus, Lucius Aemilius, 52

Rarus Sextius, Caius Cornelius, 38
Romanus, 27, 45
Rome, 17, 19, 20, 22, 23, 26, 29, 30, 33, 42
Rome, Council of, 29
Rufus, Annobal 35
Rufus, Lucius Asinius, 38
Rufus, Quintus Pomponius, 38

Sabratha, 17, 19, 20, 22-25, 27, 30, 33, 37, 48-54
    Amphitheatre, 51
    Architects, 48, 49
    Basilica, 49, 52; Justinianic, 53
    Baths, 53; Oceanus, 53; Seaward, 53
    Churches, 52, 53
    City walls, 48, 53, 54
    Colony, 49
    Curia, 52, 53
    Forum, 48-54

    Harbor, 48
    Magistrates, 19, 49, 52
    Ostia, offices at, 49
    Quarries, 48
    Temple: Antonine, 50; East Forum, 49, 51-53; of Hercules, 50, 51, 53; of Isis, 49; of Jupiter, 49, 50, 52; of Serapis, 50
    Theatre, 51, 53
    Water supply, 53
Sahara, 33
Sardinia, 31, 32
Scipio Aemilianus Minor, Publius Cornelius, 17, 25
Senate of Rome, 19, 20
Severus, 30
Severus, Alexander, 24, 25
Severus, Lucius Septimius, 24, 25, 27, 28, 41-43
Severus, Septimius, 42
Sicily, 31
Sirtic gulf, 17
Sofeggin region, 24, 25
Sofeggin, Wadi, 24, 25, 27, 33
Solomon, 31
Spain, 20, 30, 31
Stilicho, 27, 29
Suphetes, 19, 37, 42, 49

Tacapae, 37
Tacfarinas, 22
Tarhuna plateau, 23, 27, 33, 36
Tarhuna road, 36
Taxes, 20, 26, 28, 34, 42
Tebessa, 22
Thapsus, 20
Thenadassa (Ain Wif), 24
Theodosius (*magister equitum*), 27
Tiberius, 24, 35, 37
Trajan, 23, 38, 39, 49
Tripoli (*see* Oea)
Tripolitania (*see note p. 17*), 26-28, 30-32, 45, 46, 48

Troglita, John, 31
Tunisia, 24, 25, 33
Turris Tamalleni, 24

'Uqbah ibn-Nāfi', 47
Uthman, Caliph, 46
Utica (Colonia Karthago Iunonia), 17, 22

Valentinian I, 27, 46
Valentinian III, 29, 30
Vandals, 29-32, 46

Vespasian, 23, 49, 51
Vicar, 26
Vitellius, Aulus, 23

Wheat (*see* Annona), 19, 25, 26, 33

Zemzem, Wadi, 24, 25, 27, 33
Zeno, 30
Zeugitana, 31
Zintan, 24